SODOM'S SECOND COMING

F. LaGARD SMITH

SODOM'S SECOND COMING

Copyright © 1993 by Harvest House Publishers
Eugene, Oregon 97402

Library of Congress Cataloging-in-Publication Data

Smith, F. LaGard (Frank LaGard), 1944–
   Sodom's second coming / F. LaGard Smith.
     p.   cm.
   ISBN 1-56507-154-9
   1. Homosexuality—Religious aspects—Christianity. 2. Gay liberation—United States.   I. Title.
HQ76.25.S6   1993
305.9'0664—dc20   93-3487
                                      CIP

94 95 96 97 98 99 00 — 10 9 8 7 6 5 4 3

With grateful appreciation to ...

Jim Woodroof and Mark Olsen for reviewing the manuscript.

Alvin Sneed, M.D., for lending a medical eye to the text.

Robert Whelan, Stephen Green, and Colin Hart for assisting with British statistical information and other background materials.

Victor Durrington and Wendy Leece for volunteering research material.

To my mentor and friend

Homer Hailey

*who has blessed a generation of students
and even on the doorstep of ninety
remains dedicated to faithful Christian scholarship.*

Contents

CHAPTER 1

Gays at Your Doorstep

The people who are most bigoted are the people
who have no convictions at all.
—G. K. Chesterton

It's time we Christians had a frank talk about gay rights. Everyone else has: the media, the military, state legislatures, city councils, teachers' unions, local school boards—even the President of the United States. More and more people are coming to believe that homosexuals ought to have greater rights than they have ever had before.

Seen by gay activists, this decade will give new meaning to the expression "the gay nineties." They believe that future generations will look back on the 1990's as their decade, just as we now look back on the 1960's and the battle for black equality.

Already more than 75 openly gay and lesbian officials have been elected in local, state, and congressional positions. More than 130 states, counties, and cities now have gay-rights laws on the books, and a national anti-discrimination act is being drafted.

As this book goes to press, the battle over gays in the military is still far from settled. Implementation of President Clinton's compromise policy—known colloquially as "don't ask, don't tell, don't pursue"—may have left gays uncertain as to their current status. Nonetheless, most gays have been more heartened than disappointed with the executive decision, realizing that the President had an uphill battle with Congress and the military. Most gays have welcomed the partial lifting of the ban as a prelude to the day when it is lifted altogether.[1]

The fact that gays in the military—not the economy, not crime, not drug abuse—became the subject for one of the President's first executive orders upon taking office is evidence of a liberal political culture that has become preoccupied with gay rights.

What do you think about all of this? Do you feel that it is somehow unchristian not to tolerate gays? Are we being too narrow-minded, too insensitive, too unloving? And what do you think Jesus would say about today's gays?

Before you answer that last question, I should tell you that a growing number of the clergy are assuring us with great confidence that Jesus would vote for the latest gay-rights legislation.

The fact that you probably bought this book in a Christian bookstore increases the odds that you are already opposed to gay rights. So if what you are wanting me to do is to confirm what you already believe, then I'll say it right up front: Gay rights are wrong. Worse than that, gay rights are outrageous!

You can be sure that the catchphrase "gay rights" is not just the pervasive marketing of a "live-and-let-live" philosophy. As used by activist homosexuals, "gay rights" means special legal privileges for a class of people whose only common denominator is that they choose to engage in homosexual acts.

Hardly anyone stops to notice that gay rights means *heterosexuals* having to *give up* rights—like the right to consider character when renting one's house or when hiring the church secretary; or like the right of parents to keep their children from being taught that homosexual couples are just as acceptable as mommie and daddy.

Can You Articulate How You Feel?

If the gay-rights scenario alarms you, are you able to articulate *why*? Peter reminds us that we must "always be prepared to give an answer to everyone who asks... with gentleness and respect...."[2]

Sometimes the more strongly and deeply we feel about a subject, the more difficulty we have expressing our feelings. Like two-year-olds, we wish we could get away with simply saying *"Because!"* For most of us, justification for opposing the gay-rights movement seems so obvious that we find it almost impossible to believe that someone could feel any other way.

The demand for gay rights may anger us all the more because trying to respond to it is so frustrating. By its very nature, we are left speechless. When that which ought to speak for itself no longer does, most of us have nothing but gaping jaws, wondering what we could possibly say to explain what should be plain on its face.

Although other immoral acts are not precisely analogous in their nonconsensual aspect, it is as if someone were to claim that murder and rape and child abuse were morally good. What are we supposed to say? If you *have* to tell people that certain things are wrong, what are the chances of ever succeeding? "Murder is wrong because ... well, because it's *wrong!*" That ought to be good enough. Sadly, when it comes to homosexual conduct, the mere assertion of its immorality isn't good enough any longer.

You and I who oppose gay rights are being put on the defensive. We are having to defend traditional family values when such fundamental values should never have to be defended in the first place. In the eyes of a value-relative baby-boomer generation, *right* has become *wrong* and *wrong* has become *right*. Are you prepared to do battle in such a moral minefield?

Different Perspectives on Every Hand

But by no means is it a foregone conclusion that all the readers of this book oppose gay rights. Many Christians, in fact, fully support the movement for equality of sexual orientation, even if they agree that homosexual conduct itself is not God's will. If you are in this category, I hope you will find the discussion to be challenging to your thinking. In the current political and moral climate, none of us can afford to remain uninformed on the issues. And, of course, we have much to answer for. As suggested by the lyrics of a current pop song, "From a distance, God is watching us."

It is also possible that some readers are practicing homosexuals, or perhaps individuals struggling with their own sexual identity. If you happen to be in either of these groups, welcome to the dialogue. If you are open enough to admit your homosexuality, I would hope that you are also open to the possibility of persuasion.

In this regard, I think it is only fair that I be completely open and expose my own biases. There are several people in my life—students and others, much closer, whom I care about deeply—who have at one time or another engaged in homosexual conduct. One former associate and friend has been diagnosed as being HIV-positive and faces the looming prospect of dying from AIDS. At his request, I baptized him in the Pacific Ocean at dawn on a morning so resplendent that it seemed the whole creation joined in joyous celebration! It was the most poignant baptism which I have ever been privileged to share.

One by one, the questioning search of others for a peace about their sexuality has entwined together their hearts and mine. If I could snap my finger and make it happen for them, I would do so in an instant. When it comes to the men and women who fight daily battles of conscience in their quest for sexual purity, I am ready and willing to reach out. Even as a full-fledged *heterosexual*, in the past I too have known what it means to fight the daily fight against the sexual beast within me.

But I confess that, because of the pain and brokenness which homosexuality has brought to people I love, there is a great contrast in my reactions when I am suddenly faced with militant gays. Every time I see a news broadcast with the latest strident demands by homosexuals for public recognition, I want to scream back at them in outrage. I confess it's a visceral reaction that seems to jump into high gear even before my intellectual self can apply the brakes.

For me, there is a quantum leap between the moral struggler and the moral rebel. The whole scene changes when "the love that dares not speak its name" not only dares to speak but also dares to demand!

Worse yet, when I see gay-rights activists being ecclesiastically blessed by the spiritually-emasculated products of some of our nation's religious seminaries fraudulently cross-dressing as ministers of the gospel, I want to overturn the pseudo-scholarly tables of these pandering flesh-merchants and throw them out of God's holy temple!

It's exactly what I think God incarnate would have done.

In fact, I'm not so sure that God isn't already doing some serious temple-cleansing of his own. The defiant stench of sexual perversion from the streets of San Francisco and West Hollywood to the gay enclaves of Provincetown, Key West, and Fire Island must be an odious reminder to God as to just how terribly wrong free will in humankind can go. What else explains the great plague of death against those who arrogantly flaunt sexual perversion in the face of God?

AIDS: A Wakeup Call

AIDS may not be a *direct* manifestation of God's wrath against homosexuals, since thousands of drug-using adults, as well as innocent children, are dying of the disease as well; and, of course, lesbians are hardly touched by it. But it certainly ought to be a wakeup call! How can one not be reminded of Scripture's warning: "Men committed indecent acts with other men, and received in themselves the due penalty for their perversion."[3]

Talking among themselves, even gay advocates acknowledge that AIDS is a disease having special implications for homosexuals: "There have been other plagues —but this one is ours. . . ."[4]

Sin often has an interesting way of bearing within itself the seeds of its own destruction. For those who contract AIDS *because of sin* (like the hundreds of heterosexuals who died of syphilis and gonorrhea in the '30's and '40's), that of itself is a kind of divine judgment.

Have we so willingly been duped into thinking that the God of the New Testament is not the same God of the Old Testament who "rained down burning sulfur on Sodom and Gomorrah" because they "gave themselves up to sexual immorality and perversion"?[5] Or that those of us living at the dawn of the twenty-first century could never experience the deadly consequences of sin as did the 24,000 Israelites who died in a single day for having committed sexual immorality?[6]

Whether heterosexual or homosexual, have we so easily forgotten that the same Creator God who gave us human sexuality is also the Righteous Judge of the universe?

Forgivable Sinners

Oh, I haven't forgotten Jesus' reaction to the woman caught in adultery. As seen in the person of Jesus, our God is a loving and forgiving God. One thing I know: If

God can love *me* with my rebellious heart, and forgive *me* of sexual sin, then he can love and forgive *anyone*.

But I also know that Jesus told the adulterous woman to go and *sin no more*. He knew the difference between the *sinner* and the *sin*. Sadly, most of us have forgotten what it means to live a repentant, transformed life in gratitude for God's gracious and unmerited favor. Our minds can rarely accommodate both the hard preaching which the gospel sometimes demands and the tender compassion which we owe the spiritually endangered. We tend to gravitate toward the extremes of either harsh, uncaring denunciation or a soppy, nonjudgmental re-definition of sin.

And who among us these days has the moral maturity or sophistication to distinguish between concern for the individual, with all the compassion it entails, and, on a much broader scale, concern for society at large, which may call us to difficult decisions having negative impli-cations for individuals we truly care about?

On the broader societal level—the level on which the issue of gay rights is played out—the question is not what Jesus would say to a struggling homosexual. We already know the answer: "Penitent one, your sins are forgiven. Go and sin no more."

And I suspect we are on safe ground to suggest that Jesus would also say to the one whose sexual identity is in turmoil, "I know it won't be easy. What I'm asking you to do may *seem* more than you can bear."

That's the kind of loving God we have. He cares about our struggle with sin.

Gay Rights Is Another Matter

But the crucial question shouting out from the front page of the morning newspaper is, What would Jesus say in response to the militant movement for gay rights?

To get some idea of what Jesus might say if he were interviewed by today's check-out-counter tabloids, just imagine what a different response Jesus surely would have given if the adulterous woman had turned to him and said, "Sir, I don't *need* your forgiveness! I'm maritally liberated and *proud*! My family and friends have accepted me as maritally lib, and I demand that you too accept me as maritally lib. Your persistent reference to me as an 'adulteress' proves that you are a bigoted, narrow-minded, and judgmental *adulterophobe*. How dare you impose your monogamous morality on me!"

It's not so hard to imagine either the statements themselves or what Jesus' response might have been. (In other similar circumstances, Jesus always pointed to Scripture: "Haven't you read . . . ?") Except for changing the sin from adultery to homosexual acts, the statements are straight out of the six o'clock news.

We are right to be horrified at the news that some dentist has infected his unsuspecting patients with AIDS. AIDS is a plague that ought to be everyone's concern. *But so is the gay-rights movement itself.* It is a loathsome communicable disease which threatens moral values in the home, the schools, and the church. Because of gay activism, all of us are spiritually at risk.

Centuries ago, Sodom and Gomorrah represented a culture, not unlike our own, in which homosexual perversion became the very symbol of a people who had given up on God and godliness. Nothing pictured more graphically the moral depths to which a society could sink. And God sent down fire from heaven!

What we are witnessing today in the homosexual assault against America's moral values is nothing short of Sodom's second coming. And we too face God's judgment. It's time for a sober assessment, not just of activist homosexuals, but of the church, our own families, and each one of us individually. Have we, like Lot, "pitched our tents toward Sodom"?

CHAPTER 2

The Not-So-Hidden Gay Agenda

Gore said, "Come on, show him your underwear, anything goes. This is the Clinton administration." So I showed the president my underwear in the Oval Office.

—Paul Begala,
adviser to Bill Clinton

Is it possible that, even as you read these words, there are gay-rights activists sitting around in boardrooms or bathhouses furtively conspiring against the American culture? As a criminal law professor who knows what it takes to prove a criminal conspiracy, I'm not one who generally favors conspiracy theories. But it is clear that somebody out there is orchestrating the gay-rights crusade. Somebody, or a group of somebodies, is zealously pursuing a course of action aimed at the homosexualization of America.

It's not happening by accident. Somebody is organizing the Gay Pride marches and convincing the mayors of big cities to participate. Somebody else is sitting behind a computer drafting the latest gay-rights initiative for the upcoming city or statewide election. There are teachers all across America who are discussing over coffee what would be the best way to expose your sons and daughters to the moral acceptability of a gay lifestyle.

Whether any of these people are working directly in

concert, or only indirectly in sympathy with each other, we may never know. But there is one thing you can count on: *There is a gay-rights network in which many minds are working overtime to advance the goals of the gay-rights movement.*

For over two decades, much behind-the-scenes maneuvering has been going on. Consider, for example, the 1972 Gay Rights Platform drawn up by the National Coalition of Gay Organizations.[1] Among the Coalition's goals were the following:

- Repeal of all laws prohibiting private sexual acts involving consenting persons.
- Repeal of all laws prohibiting prostitution, both male and female.
- Repeal of all laws governing the age of sexual consent.
- Repeal of all legislative provisions that restrict the sex or number of persons entering into a marriage unit; and the extension of legal benefits to all persons who cohabit, regardless of sex or numbers.
- Enactment of legislation so that child custody, adoption, visitation rights, foster parenting, and the like shall not be denied because of sexual orientation or marital status.
- Encouragement and support for sex-education courses, prepared and taught by gay women and men, presenting homosexuality as a valid, healthy preference and lifestyle as a viable alternative to heterosexuality.

If you are finding some comfort in knowing that, two decades later, a substantial portion of their platform has yet to be realized, consider the success of another of their planks which 20 years ago would have been considered unthinkable, but now reads like the leading story in a current issue of *Time* magazine:

- Issuance by the President of an executive order prohibiting the military from excluding for reasons of their sexual orientation, persons who desire entrance into the Armed Services; and from issuing less-than-fully-honorable discharges for homosexuality; and the upgrading to fully honorable all such discharges previously issued, with retroactive benefits.

As we will see in a later chapter, the sex-education plank has also had growing success in some parts of the country, as has the plank relating to homosexual parenting and adoption. Had the Labour Party won the last election in Britain, they were pledged to reduce the age of consent for homosexuals from 21 to 16. Might this be a portent of what could happen soon on this side of the Atlantic? (You can bet that NAMBLA, the North American Man-Boy Love Association, is hoping so.)

Never underestimate the resolve or initiative of gay-rights activists. They have not hidden their sordid light under a bushel. The evidence of a premeditated, long-range gay-rights agenda is compelling—topped off by the election of a President from whom they now expect—and are getting—repayment in kind.

That is why it is so important that we examine the strategy and tactics of the movement. If gay-rights advocates are successful, then two decades from now we could be facing legalized prostitution, both male and female; the complete legalization of homosexual relations even with children; legal marriages for gays; parents losing custody of their children for disapproving of homosexual behavior; and even churches convicted of "hate crimes" for preaching that homosexual behavior is a sin.

The 12-Step Gay Agenda

With that grim prospect in mind, we turn now to a closer examination of the gay movement's 12-step agenda:

1. Boldly claim freedom from social restraint and demand independence from the moral order.
2. Associate homosexuals with others in order to achieve legitimacy.
3. Depict decent folks with traditional family values to be the bad guys.
4. Promote the proven lie that gays constitute 10 percent of the population, so that there is legitimacy through sheer numbers.
5. Confuse the terminology so that no one realizes the difference between sexual orientation and sexual behavior.
6. Enlist science and medicine in a bogus search for some genetic cause for homosexual behavior.
7. Don't let anyone know what it is that gays actually do sexually.
8. Find creative ways to sidestep what the Bible teaches about homosexual conduct.
9. Open the door to the church and get its blessing for homosexual expression.
10. Break down legal restrictions against sodomy and instead establish legal restrictions against discrimination.
11. Dismantle the American family and make it possible for gays to marry and adopt children.
12. Perpetuate myths about heterosexual AIDS so that the disease becomes a political asset for the gay movement.

Step One: Boldly claim freedom from social restraint and demand independence from the moral order.

For homosexuals, this first crucial step is what "coming out" has been about. Before "coming out," homosexuals were collectively and individually suffocating in the seclusion of closeted guilt. As long as their homosexuality was still in the closet, there could be no relief from the guilt, no sense of moral freedom, no claim of legitimacy.

But that's mostly in the past. For today's homosexuals, the gay closet has become a relic of an unenlightened era. First one, then another, then homosexuals by the thousands have now stepped forward with ever-increasing boldness, throwing off the shackles of societal disapproval and asserting their sexuality with the fervor of political revolutionaries. Firing their first volley in the infamous 1969 Stonewall riot in New York's Greenwich Village, militant homosexuals signaled their Declaration of Sexual Independence and established themselves as a nation within a nation. "Gay and proud" became their anthem, and "gay rights" the banner to which they pledged their allegiance.

Like the self-righteous Pharisees of Jesus' day who boldly asserted their religious freedom in the face of his condemnation, today's homosexual crusaders proclaim their freedom as if it were an Emancipation Proclamation from slavery. Yet the promise of moral freedom for gays is merely illusive. What gays fail to appreciate is that in their self-proclaimed freedom they have become even more enslaved to their own passions.

That's what Jesus was telling the Pharisees in John chapter 8: "I tell you the truth, everyone who sins is a slave to sin."[2] And that is his message even today for those who would press for unrestricted sexual expression of any kind: No matter how loudly we declare our freedom, we are still shackled to whatever passions maintain their power over us.

All the more is that true when we dare to claim liberation from the moral order itself. It's one thing to *violate* the moral order through human weakness—something which all of us do. It's another thing altogether to *deny its authority over us.* It is here, in the attempt at moral emancipation, that gay activists tragically fool themselves into thinking they are free.

However much we might wish to deny it, the moral order has a way of keeping us in its grip even at the very moment we refuse to acknowledge its existence. We may *feel* free, as if we were astronauts floating in outer space. But, like them, we are tethered, whether we like it or not. And of course we ought to *like* it, for our tether is also our lifeline. Isn't that what Jesus was saying? Feeling sexually free without a moral tether is an invitation to sure destruction. Being free at the end of a morally-legitimate lifeline is being *free indeed!*

The gay-rights claim of moral freedom is a myth. That one small step out of the closet for homosexuals is one giant step toward certain disaster for both homosexuals and society at large.

Step Two: Associate homosexuals with others in order to achieve legitimacy.

In John chapter 8, Jesus was confronted by snobbish religious leaders who rested their personal righteousness on their heritage as descendants of Abraham. "How could we be religiously wrong as long as we are Abraham's descendants?" they were asking.

The gay-rights movement has ingeniously adopted a number of different ways to follow the same ploy. The idea is to somehow associate themselves with groups of heterosexuals who are unquestionably accepted throughout society, in the hope that they themselves will thereby be accepted. So far the tactic is working better than they ever could have imagined.

Just Another "Community"?

Perhaps more subtle than some of the more articulated arguments is the frequent reference to "the gay community."

The *"gay community"*? You mean, like the *black* community? The *Hispanic* community? The *Christian* community?

While no one would deny that there is a segment of society made up of homosexuals sharing common interests—and therefore a "community" in that sense—if gays can somehow be linked with the many *legitimate* communities which make up our society, their hope is that homosexuality itself might appear to take on the same legitimacy as, for instance, race or national heritage. Of course, that link is as patently contrived as if an attempt were made to confer legitimate status to the "adulterous community," or to the "tax-fraud community," or to the "white-collar-crime community."

Equally subtle is the hiding place that one might hope to find in the midst of a "community." Whereas we rightly assess personal moral character only in the case of individuals, we normally think of communities in a morally neutral sense. In "the black community," for example, one can find both moral and immoral members of the community. The same goes for "the white community," "the Hispanic community," and so on.

However, when an entire community's identity is based solely upon its unique moral character, the implication is all too clear: If there can somehow be a sanitized, legitimized "gay community," then the individuals who make up that community can automatically be considered morally legitimate as well. Instead of *guilt* by association, there is a hoped-for *legitimacy* by association.

Just Another Civil-Rights Group?

Never is legitimacy by association more coveted than when the gay-rights movement attempts to link itself with truly legitimate civil-rights movements. Every effort is made by homosexuals to ride piggyback on the fortunes of blacks, women, and other legitimate minority groups. But minority groups must never be confused with special-interest groups.

As for minority groups, we champion laws prohibiting discrimination against race, gender, and national origin because they represent a status over which their members have no choice. Naturally, that raises one of the most crucial questions in the entire debate: whether homosexuals have any choice in the matter. (The issue will be more fully developed in later chapters.)

Suffice it to say for now that the burden is on the gay-rights movement to establish that homosexual conduct is *not* volitionally chosen. In that regard, their persistent reference to "sexual *preference*" and "gay *lifestyle*" betrays their attempt to deny personal volition in their sexual practices. Legitimate minority status is a bogus claim by what amounts to nothing more than a special-interest group.

Of course, gay activists point out that we also have laws prohibiting discrimination on the basis of *religion*, wherein one's faith is personally chosen. But the attempted analogy still misses the mark, because religion is a matter of Constitutionally protected belief. Religious *belief* stands in sharp contrast to homosexual *behavior*, which the Supreme Court has specifically declared not to be Constitutionally protected.

The Pro-Choice, Pro-Gay Connection

Far less lofty than the efforts which are made to mimic legitimate minorities is the well-documented liaison between gay-rights groups and pro-choice, pro-abortion organizations. If ever there were an unholy alliance, this is it! Considering the fact that homosexuals will never have to worry about the unwanted pregnancy that leads to abortion, it gives new meaning to the saying that politics makes strange bedfellows. How strange indeed!

More importantly, instead of providing gay activists with added moral legitimacy by association with a high-profile social cause, it simply confirms how morally perverse their movement is. Pro-choice for the "men of conscience," as they are called by their pro-abortion allies, only serves to put gays in league with yet another special-interest group desperately seeking moral freedom where none exists. How much more morally bankrupt can gays be than when they are willing to trade on the lives of 1.5 million aborted babies a year in order to gain public approval of their own homosexual lifestyle!

Ironically, there is already expressed consternation over the potential convergence of two separately developing streams: 1) Gay-initiated efforts to find a "biological determinant" for homosexuality, wherein homosexual orientation is the product of perinatal chemical configurations in utero; and 2) the growing practice of eugenic abortions that would permit concerned parents to abort any fetus indicating homosexual tendencies.

Even though discovery of a "biological determinant" is about as likely as meeting Shirley MacLaine in a future lifetime, gays find themselves in the same embarrassing dilemma as feminists, who demand unrestricted choice, yet are offended when that choice results in the methodical slaughter of female fetuses in sex-selection abortions.

Once one jumps the moral cue, he has to be careful in his choice of allies. The *"immoral* order"—and there is one—tends to be as integrative and interdependent as is the *moral* order.

Parading Celebrity Comrades

Among the more visible tactics of gay-rights advocates is their concerted effort to surround themselves in a show of strength with every important personage they can muster, whether it be politicians, entertainment celebrities, athletes, or even religious leaders.

The strategy is no secret. We have it from their own pens:

> Our campaign should not overlook the Celebrity Endorsement. The celebrities in question can, of course, be either straight or gay ... but must always be well liked and respected by the public.
>
> If homosexual, the celebrity jams homo-hatred by presenting a favorable gay image at odds with the stereotype. If straight, the spokesperson (who deserves the Medal of Valor) provides the public with an impressive role model of social tolerance to emulate. In either case, the psychological response among straights is the same, and lays the groundwork for conversion:
>
> I like and admire Mr. Celeb;
> Mr. Celeb is queer and/or respects queers;
> so either I must stop liking and admiring Mr. Celeb,
> or else it must be all right for me to respect queers.[3]

Naturally, many of the big names that are paraded before us are homosexuals recognized and admired for their outstanding talent. Consider conductor/composer Leonard Bernstein[4] and tennis stars Billie Jean King and Martina Navratilova, to name but three.

But it is the *heterosexual* celebrities who better serve the movement's goal of achieving public acceptability. Simply consider the recent uproar over Colorado's initiative to prevent special gay-rights ordinances, and what you see is a virtual Who's Who of America's top entertainers coming to the defense of the gays. The list is long, including Barbara Streisand, Lily Tomlin, Whoopi Goldberg, Joan Rivers, Cher, Liza Minnelli, and Sidney Poitier. John Denver got in on the act by sponsoring a concert to raise 50,000 dollars in an effort to repeal the initiative.

Even former President (and Sunday school teacher) Jimmy Carter defended his boycott-breaking appearance in Colorado by saying that his visit would help the people who were fighting that law.[5]

Sadly, there has never been a greater friend and benefactor of the gay movement than our current President. His association with homosexual activist David Mixner is well-known. It was Mixner who marshaled the army of gays that helped elect Clinton, and the same Mr. Mixner who persuaded his friend in the nation's highest office to declare the army of gays in the Army official. (It was also Mixner who said he became "literally sick to my stomach" when Clinton suggested that the military might have some legitimate concerns after all.)[6]

Mixner's important political connection did not go unrewarded. During the frenzy of Clinton's many inaugural celebrations, The Gay and Lesbian Victory Fund saluted Mixner with an inaugural ball. It was attended by a host of luminaries, among whom were actress Sigourney Weaver; White House spokesman George Stephanopoulos; three California senators, including Diane Feinstein, Barbara Boxer, and Alan Cranston (now retired); and singers Gladys Knight, Patti Austin, and Peter, Paul, and Mary.

It was a sign of the times, and of the growing public acceptability of the gay movement, when the Lesbian and Gay Bands of America played in the inaugural parade while Girl Scouts handed out American flags and AIDS ribbons.

If the gays ever wanted a calling card, they have it in the current President. "Bill Clinton is the Abraham Lincoln of the lesbian and gay community," said Gregory

King, a spokesman for the Human Rights Campaign Fund, a pro-gay political group whose 75,000 members raised 2.5 million dollars for the Clinton campaign.[7]

"Being gay is a plus, because the president's looking for diversity," said Andrew Barrer, director of Coalition '93, an organization set up to push gay and lesbian candidates for federal appointments.[8]

On every side, gays have gained support from people of influence. The associations which they have carefully cultivated for over two decades have brought them a level of public acceptability that one could never have dreamed of happening in so short a time.

Of course, legitimacy by association misses the issue altogether. If you live by association you can also die by association. Would the gay-rights movement wish us to associate them with homosexual serial killers Elmer Wayne Henley, John Wayne Gacy, Juan Corona, Wayne Williams, and Jeffrey Dahmer?[9]

A Genealogy for Gays?

Yet not even the impressive list of sympathetic luminaries seems sufficient for gays. Have you heard all the historical revision going on lately? One after another, historical figures are being "outed" as homosexuals. The latest coup, if it is to be believed, is "gay-hater" and former FBI chief J. Edgar Hoover, who according to biographer Anthony Summers (*Official and Confidential: The Secret Life of J. Edgar Hoover*) was homosexually involved with his assistant director, and even dallied with being a transvestite on occasion.

But just look at the revisionist strategy and why gays correctly perceive the reasons for its success:

> The honor roll of prominent gay or bisexual men and women is truly eye-popping. From Socrates to Eleanor Roosevelt, Tchaikovsky to

Bessie Smith, Alexander the Great to Alexander Hamilton, and Leonardo da Vinci to Walt Whitman, the list of suspected "inverts" is old hat to us but surprising news to heterosexual America.

Famous historical figures are especially useful to us for two reasons: first, they are invariably dead as a doornail, hence in no position to deny the truth and sue for libel. Second, and more serious, the virtues and accomplishments that make these historic gay figures admirable cannot be gainsaid or dismissed by the public, since high school history textbooks have already set them in incontrovertible cement.[10]

Apparently it has become particularly important in the debate over gays in the military to dredge up great military figures of the past: Julius Caesar; the entire army of Sparta; Lord Kitchener, Frederick the Great, Alexander the Great (as mentioned), and so on.

London columnist Frank Johnson suggests, tongue in cheek, that, given the preference for anyone with "the Great" after his or her name, it's surely only a matter of time before Catherine the Great is "outed" as a lesbian![11]

And who's to know the difference? With none of them around to defend themselves, even George Washington, Napoleon, and General Patton aren't safe.

As a matter of historical fact, Frederick the Great and Kitchener probably *were* homosexuals. But apparently Alexander the Great was guilty of no greater crime than the male, Platonic friendship in which the ancient world was more interested than in the sexual craving of our own time.

Caesar, of course, was married, and spent a good deal of time with Cleopatra. Whether this precluded other, homosexual liaisons is by no means clear. But until there is more evidence, the gay-rights movement is no more entitled to him than is the other side.[12]

In all of the frenzy for establishment of a gay pedigree, it seems to be lost on gay activists that they are committing the same sin which they condemn in heterosexuals: defining a homosexual by his homosexuality. Are historical figures to be admired *because of* their homosexuality, or are they to be admired for having accomplished what they did *despite* their homosexuality?

Acceptability Through Sympathy

A final way in which the gay movement succeeds in gaining public support is not a tactic which I would guess anyone is cynical enough to purposely exploit. It just works out that way. I refer here, of course, to the many AIDS-related deaths which have seen one celebrity after another go to his grave prematurely.

It is considered indelicate to mention it, but certain sports, like men's ice-skating, have felt the brunt of AIDS more than others. The obituary in Canada alone includes such top skaters as Rob McCall, Brian Pockar, Dennis Coi, and Shaun McGill. There is also Britain's John Curry. Add to that list Ondrej Nepla, the 1972 Olympic gold medalist from Czechoslovakia, who has already died, and now Barry Hagen, the World Champion ice dancer in 1982 and 1983, who has tested positive to the HIV virus, and you begin to realize how devastating the gay lifestyle can be, even in a single sport.

On another front, who hasn't been appalled by the loss of so many people with creative talent in the field of arts and entertainment? In the past decade there have been so many funerals in Hollywood that, as one gay put it, "I'm simply weary from attending them." Many of those who died were relatively unknown behind-the-scenes writers, choreographers, and dancers. Others have been superstars whose deaths have touched us all.

For example, who among us didn't admire the strength and gracefulness that permitted Rudolf Nureyev to leap in exquisite slow motion? Or enjoy the cinematic roles played by Rock Hudson? I still remember the days of early television and the popular show-biz flair of Liberace. These people are gone now, robbed of life by the homosexual lifestyle which they shared in common. Yet they have become the heroes of the hour.

One might have thought that these tragic deaths would have been an embarrassment to the gay-rights movement. But every cause needs its martyrs, and none could be more suited for the gay movement than deaths which, in one stroke, combine unprecedented public sympathy and celebrity-status homosexuality. What could be better than legitimacy by association unless perhaps it is legitimacy by sympathy?

The connection is not difficult to draw. Were you shocked to learn how Rock Hudson died? If so, how could you possibly oppose gay rights? Hudson was a homosexual, you know.

Were you grieved at the loss which Nureyev's death brought to the world of ballet? If so, what could possibly be wrong with gay rights? Nureyev was a homosexual, you know.

No one should underestimate the strength of the sympathy vote. In the midst of all the cynical attempts to gain public acceptability through contrived associations with legitimate minorities, civil-rights movements, and supportive celebrities, nothing grabs the American people quite like the association between AIDS and gay rights.

When faced with death, we often find a common bond that we never knew in life. In death we are neither homosexual nor heterosexual. And that is a comforting thought to the gay movement, because it means that society will tend to look more kindly upon the special risk that homosexual men face—and thus more kindly upon their movement for social recognition.

The fact that homosexuals have virtually absolute control over that risk hardly seems to matter. For every person who blames homosexuals for the AIDS epidemic and its threat even to young innocents, there are another two or more people who let their sympathy for AIDS victims cloud the quite separate issue of gay rights.

I say "quite separate," but perhaps in another vein we would do well to make the very connection that gays would love us to make. After all, were it not for the movement for gay rights, in several decades the tragedy of the AIDS epidemic for homosexuals and many more innocents in America could literally be ancient history.

As we leave steps one and two in the gay movement's agenda, each of the remaining ten steps will be covered chapter by chapter. One of the most crucial aspects of the agenda is step three, in which gay activists attempt to turn the spotlight off themselves and make the rest of us look like the bad guys. Because most of us want to be "the good guys in the white hats," the finger-pointing, table-turning tactic has been extremely successful. But it's time we put the spotlight back where it belongs. As God's people, we have no reason to be on the defensive. The moral high ground is always ours.

CHAPTER 3

Homophobia and Other Finger-Pointing

"Let me tell you, Mary, if you've met one low-class, mongoloid, rednecked, hair-backed, potbellied, stereotyping bigot, you've met them all."
—Often heard in
Boston-area gay bars[1]

To use a variation of the old saying, Once I couldn't even *spell* "homophobic," and now I *are* one! Where in the world did this awful-sounding and mis-aimed word *homophobic* ever come from? Anything that is a phobia just *sounds* bad! Whatever its source, nothing has been more successful in misframing the current issues than the non-issue of "homophobia."

As an implied motive for opposing the gay-rights movement, what could be sillier? There's no *fear* to it, as "phobia" suggests. We do not fear either what homosexuals do in private or our own sexuality, as if suddenly someday out of the blue we might wake up and be homosexuals ourselves.

There is only one sense in which homophobia has any real meaning, and in that sense only I admit to having been homophobic *for a night!* It's a long story, but on a trip through Italy one summer I experienced my first earthquake and was sexually accosted by the local hotel manager all in the same evening.

I distinctly remember being in a great quandary, wondering whether to leave the door unlocked so that I could run out of the room if there was another tremor, or whether to lock the door to keep him out! Despite being definitely homophobic throughout the rest of the night, *earthquake*ophobia won out! Fortunately, the lecherous manager never reappeared, and as I walked out of the hotel the next morning, my homophobia went into remission, never to surface again.

Gay authors Marshall Kirk and Hunter Madsen agree that homophobia is a red herring—and a dangerous one from their perspective. Instead of our being *fearful* of gays, they believe that we *hate* them! They therefore propose that we ought to be called "homohaters" instead.[2] I don't know. That label may be more accurate from their perspective, but I can guarantee you that it would never be nearly as successful as *homophobia*. When you've got homophobia, you generally foam at the mouth, don't you?

In fairness to the gay movement, it must be admitted that there *is* some "homohatred" out there. That's where all the gay-bashing comes from: from undesirable elements in society who would beat up on little children at the movies if they thought they could get away with it!

It's not just gays these animals hate. It's anyone who might give them an excuse for not being on the bottom rung of society, where they themselves belong. If they can demean *any* class of people as being lower than themselves, then they can fool themselves into thinking that they are not really the lowest of the low. But these folks are not your average heterosexual next-door neighbors with 2.3 kids and a dog.

Likewise, in fairness to those of us who oppose the gay movement on grounds of conscience, it must be said that we do *not* hate homosexuals. Homosexuals don't often appreciate the distinction (or perhaps *trust* it), but we truly *do* know the difference between sin and sinner. And we truly *do* love the sinner. How could we not? We too are all sinners!

However, if we're honest about it, we Christians have not always *acted* as if we truly loved the homosexual sinner. If we do have a phobia, it's probably "accept-aphobia." We sometimes fear that any acceptance of penitent homosexuals in the church will lead to a perceived softness on the sin itself. And that attitude is clearly wrong!

If what gays are talking about when they refer to fear and hatred is the *anger* we often feel—and sometimes express—then I, for one, plead guilty. But it's not personalized anger at individual homosexuals. My anger is outrage at the gay movement and the immorality it represents. My anger is at the influence it is having on people I love. My anger is at seeing the moral foundations of my country crumbling around me because we have lost either the ability or the will to be moral people.

Angry? You bet! But *hate* homosexuals? No. *Fear* homosexuals? Why should I? The only true homophobes I know are the politicians who see the gay lobby coming and run scared!

Disrespect Breeds Disrespect

If activist homosexuals are serious about wanting society's respect for homosexuals, they must realize how misguided they have been in trying to win that respect. It may be understandable that gays are outraged by the apparent success of the religious right, whom they consider to be bigoted hatemongers. But is it possible that there might be legitimate opposition to their cause from thoughtful people who value tolerance and individual privacy as much as they do? What is it, exactly, that prompts so many people (not just Christians) to oppose the gay-rights movement?

Surely it can't be simply the AIDS epidemic, because antihomosexual sentiment was around long before there was AIDS. Nor can opposition be exclusively laid at the

feet of organized religion. Consider the low level of tolerance for homosexuals in former Soviet bloc countries, in
which for decades atheism has been the official party
line.

Perhaps there is the matter of violence when homosexuals don't get what they want. Gay-rights activists win
few friends among heterosexuals who might disagree
with the governor in their state signing into law some
controversial tax measure, but who would never consider pelting him with rotten eggs.

And what of the double standards? Opposing homosexuality is a "hate crime," but labeling people as "ho-
mophobics" and "religious bigots" somehow is *not*?

Yet there are more complex reasons for the heterosexual backlash, beginning with the hypocrisy of intolerance by homosexuals. It seems not to matter to gays that
having to hire a homosexual might infringe on someone
else's religious faith—the free expression of which is a
right specifically guaranteed by the Constitution. Lately,
demands by homosexuals for legal recognition have
made a quantum leap from *no right at all* to a *super-right*
squelching all others! Is subtle *inverse discrimination* somehow more virtuous than open discrimination? Should
their *intolerance* be expected to beget our *tolerance*?

"Discrimination Against Gays" may be the headline,
but the real issue is hidden in fine print. In most states,
homosexual conduct is not a crime. Even in states where
it is, there are no bedroom police invading anyone's
sexual privacy, and few employers raise an eyebrow as
long as one's sexual preferences are left at home. Yet that
is not enough. What homosexuals want is not simply
legal recognition but *moral sanction*. How better to quiet
one's conscience and morally justify an immoral act than
by getting public approval through law?

Goodness knows that heterosexuals are involved in
plenty of fornicating and adultery. Yet few would have
the audacity to force society to *officially* condone sexual

practices which are still frowned upon in an era of almost unrestrained sexual freedom. It is the brazenness of the gay movement in attempting to force official recognition which affronts other people. Being asked to understand moral failings is one thing; being forced to accept *immorality* as if it were *moral* is quite another.

With moral values everywhere in rapid retreat, even the irreligious have cause for concern. There is only so much blurring of fundamental right and wrong that we can be asked to accept, and gay rights stretches us beyond the limit. Gay rights has become a key battleground precisely because, with homosexual behavior being the issue, the stark difference between right and wrong will rarely be clearer.

There is a sense in which the gay movement *literally* symbolizes our inability to distinguish right from wrong. When one gender says to another gender, "I don't need you," it nullifies the separateness of gender and the significant differences which gender celebrates. Misogyny (a denial of need for womanhood) becomes androgyny (a neutered sameness).

As a society of moral actors, it is *moral androgyny*—the inability to distinguish "moral" from "immoral"—that we fear. We are not *homo*phobic, but *ambiguo*phobic. We fear any further ambiguity in matters of morals, and we reject being forced to redefine right and wrong as if there were no difference between the two. If something as blatant as sex between two people of the same gender is not definitively wrong, then all moral standards are up for grabs.

When "gay rights" appears on some future ballot initiative, discrimination in housing or hiring will not be the issue. The real issue will be whether we will allow a minority of those who can no longer distinguish "moral" from "immoral" to force the rest of us to give up our own

ability to discriminate between right and wrong whenever we encounter that choice being flaunted in our
faces.

Is Nature Itself Homophobic?

When the gay movement insists that everyone who
disagrees with them is prejudiced, narrow-minded, or,
worse yet, a fundamentalist Christian, they misjudge—
even underestimate—their adversaries. There are count-
less individuals from various walks of life who fit none of
these caricatures, and yet find homosexual conduct
repugnant.

Why should that be? It is worth considering a rather
overlooked reason—that *nature itself* has given humankind an aversion to homosexuality. Nature gives all
species instincts for the express purpose of the preservation of that species. Does it not make sense, then, that
nature also gives instincts which support the procreation and continuation of the human race?

Most heterosexuals, without any religious concern
whatsoever, find that same-sex practices make their
skin crawl. Is such a reaction simply a societal conditioning, as the gay movement would have us believe? Or is
this "conditioning" a built-in directive of nature?

For all the millions of "closet" heterosexuals who
reject the gay lifestyle, yet wear a facade of tolerant
acceptance for fear of being branded as prejudiced hatemongers, there is this to consider: If the repugnance
engendered by homosexual behavior is an inherent natural response, shouldn't it be embraced?

Just because we find something repugnant doesn't
mean that we are prejudiced or hateful. (Are we prejudiced or hateful when we find ourselves repulsed by
crime and violence?) What it means is that *we are giving
recognition and validation to our basic instincts which warn us
of obvious danger.*

There is no reason for any of us to be homophobic or hateful. Like the rest of us, homosexuals as individuals are all God's creatures. But we would do well to seriously contemplate whether *nature itself* might not be naturally homophobic.[3]

Shifting the Blame

Adam did it. Children do it. Co-felons specialize in it. It's the ancient art of finger-pointing. This art is most often observed when someone has been backed into a corner and there is no way out. It's all about guilt and creatively attempting to avoid the consequences. Sometimes it's called by other names, like "turning the tables" or "shifting the blame."

It's a terrorist tactic ("We've been oppressed") and the rioters' favorite defense ("We're victims of an unjust society"). Perhaps you've used it yourself ("But, officer, everyone else was driving just as fast").

Shifting the blame has become an art form on America's campuses. It's all about "political correctness." Dare take a conservative position on any issue declared off-limits by the liberal establishment, and you will be accused of discrimination, intolerance, hatred, and bigotry. The goal is unobstructed "diversity"—including, of course, sexual orientation. (The University of Arizona takes sensitivity to the limits, penalizing any perceived discrimination on the basis of *individual style*, whatever that is![4]

To promote diversity, the University of Wisconsin-Milwaukee handed out a list of 49 "Ways to Experience Diversity," which urged students to "Hold hands publicly with someone of a different race or *someone of the same sex as you*."[5] On the all-women campus of Smith College, the powers that be define the crime of "heterosexism" to include "not acknowledging their [gay's] existence." Dare refuse to hold hands with someone of your own gender, or dare refuse to acknowledge the legitimacy of gays, and you risk being arrested by the sensitivity police. *You* become the offender, not those who break all the moral rules.

It's not just rhetoric and empty threats. All this homo-phobia-phobia can literally get you kicked off campus! At the University of Michigan, a student was brought up on charges of sexual harassment when he suggested that a counseling plan could be developed for helping gays become straight.[6]

When it comes to political correctness and gays, it is often based upon incredibly sensitive sensitivity. It doesn't get more paranoid than when gay students bad-gered New York University Law School into canceling a moot-court argument which was to have presented the question of child custody rights for lesbians. One might think that lesbians would have welcomed discussion of the issue as a matter of consciousness-raising. But, no, they complained that "writing arguments [against the right of lesbians to win custody] is hurtful to a group of people and this is hurtful to all of us."[7] And who was held responsible for their thin-skinned paranoia? You guessed it—those who had been so insensitive as not to consider how hurtful it would be to argue *both* sides of a legitimate legal question. How dare they!

We Are in Good Company

It didn't happen on a campus, but not even Jesus escaped being the victim of finger-pointing and blame-shifting. John chapter 8 is a textbook illustration of how the tactic works. You'll recall that Jesus was locked in heated debate with the Pharisees over the issue of what constitutes spiritual freedom. (Sound familiar?) Jesus had just said something about *truth* and the fact that, in rejecting truth, these pretentious religious leaders be-longed to their father, the devil.[8]

Naturally Jesus' words were politically incorrect and did not go down well with the Pharisees. They knew that Jesus had them perfectly pegged, so what else could they possibly do? They were in a corner. They had no alternative. It was time for some serious finger-pointing and blame-shifting.

Should we be surprised, then, that they tried to turn the tables? To the Lord of the universe—God himself incarnate—these pious pretenders sniveled weakly, "Aren't we right in saying that you are a Samaritan and demon-possessed?"[9]

They might just as well have accused him of being a narrow-minded religious bigot. Or clergyphobic!

It would have been nice if at least they could have gotten their facts straight. Jesus was neither demon-possessed nor a Samaritan—the latter fact being easily subject to verification had they chosen to do even the slightest research. But, then, that's the nature of finger-pointing: It often gets its facts wrong, and usually exactly backward. As we have already seen, there is simply no evidence that adverse reaction to the gay movement has anything to do with either fear or hatred.

Shifting the Blame Perpetuates Discord

What I find most distressing about being labeled homophobic is that the labeling short-circuits any meaningful discussion. It means that we can never get to the important issues. Of course, that's the whole purpose of the name-calling. It's a defense mechanism to be used when the argument is all but lost.

When gays hurl their invectives against (in particular) Christians, they end up doing the very thing that they accuse Christians of doing: unfairly labeling them. The difference is that Christians directly address the issue at hand: the unacceptability of homosexual behavior.

Drawing from basic moral principles, Christians can legitimately say to homosexuals, "What you are doing is

wrong." Gays, on the other hand, must content themselves with manufacturing something that merely *sounds*
bad—like homophobia. The label not only gets the facts
wrong, but also has absolutely nothing to do with whether
gays deserve the social recognition which they covet.
Even if they were right about heterosexuals being fearful
of gays, it would say nothing about the morality of their
cause.

Finally, the charge of homophobia is supremely spu-
rious because it undermines the sincere concern felt by
those who object to the gay agenda. Far from opposing
human rights, as accused, the goal of Christians is human dignity.

Will homosexuals never believe us when we say that
we are genuinely concerned about a gay lifestyle which
is self-destructive? Naturally, it's all right for gays to talk
freely among themselves about the high incidence of
alcoholism, drug addiction, and suicide among homosexuals. But are the rest of us to be shut out of the
discussion only because we suggest that the gay lifestyle
itself is the cause of all the misery?

And if gays can express their anger about the "wrongness" of intolerance against them, are we completely off
base to be concerned about a society which has become
so tolerant that it risks losing all sense of "wrongness"?

Tolerating homosexual behavior makes us moral handi-
caps, unable to distinguish right and wrong in other
crucial areas of social interaction. America simply will
not survive if something so obviously wrong as homosexual behavior becomes morally acceptable.

We have no reason to hate or fear homosexuals as a
class of individuals. But in giving public recognition to
gay rights, it is only at great personal and national peril
that we lose our ability to discriminate between right and
wrong.

CHAPTER 4

Ten Percent Gay: The Big Lie

When war is declared, Truth is the first casualty.
—Arthur Ponsonby
(first Baron Ponsonby
of Shulbrede)

Ask almost anyone today—including Christians—the percentage of homosexuals in the general population and the figure you get immediately is "10 percent." Compute that against the general U.S. population of 250 million (as of the 1990 census), and what you would have is a giant closet filled with 25 *million* homosexuals—very nearly as many homosexuals as blacks in America (30 million) and Hispanics (22 million).

Keep working with the 25 million gay estimate, and we supposedly have almost as many homosexuals in the United States as the 29 million population of California. (And what could be a better barometer of gays than California!) Taking a more international perspective, there would be as many homosexuals in America as the *total* population of Austria, Denmark, Ireland, and Sweden *combined*. Can that really be? Who says so?

The Kinsey Rumor

You have probably heard of the Kinsey surveys which surfaced in the forties and fifties. The infamous "10 percent gay" figure originated from Kinsey's reports,

"Sexual Behavior in the Human Male" (1948) and "Sexual Behavior in the Human Female (1953). The reports have been accepted almost uncritically ever since then. What is just now being acknowledged by experts across the board—regardless of bias—is that Kinsey's surveys were not scientific in nature, and were never really intended to be.

Having been assigned to teach a course in sexuality, Kinsey discovered that there was a dearth of information on the subject of sexual practices. He therefore began an informal survey by asking neighbors across the back fence about their sex lives. From there he proceeded mostly to institutional populations, like schools, prisons, and hospitals. Because of his limited sample groups —which did not include large segments of the general population, either ethnically, sociologically, or geographically—any extrapolations of his findings were seriously flawed.

At best, the 10 percent homosexual figure says nothing more than that 10 percent of Kinsey's *particular sample* were homosexuals. (A survey conducted in a gay bar might well result in something near 100 percent gay!) "It's just not a real number," says University of Washington sociologist Pepper Schwartz.[1]

Adding to the difficulties with the Kinsey figures is the ambiguity in his reports as to what constituted homosexuality and homosexual behavior. His attention to psychotic reactions, not simply homosexual experience, means that in many cases "merely thinking about homosexuality turns the person into a Kinsey homosexual."[2]

Newsweek's Patrick Rogers reports that "new evidence [beyond Kinsey] suggests that ideology, not sound science, has perpetuated a 1-in-10 myth. In the nearly half-century since Kinsey, no survey has come close to duplicating his findings. Most recent surveys place gays and lesbians at somewhere between 1 and 3 percent of the population. While experts say these survey results are biased by underreporting from reticent participants, the gap is still significant."[3]

Irresistible Propaganda

So how did it happen that Kinsey's 10 percent figure got so much public airtime? Marshall Kirk and Hunter Madsen, writing for a gay audience in *After the Ball*, have let the cat out of the bag with this admission: "Based on their personal experience, most straights probably would put the gay population at 1% or 2% of the general population. Yet . . . when straights are asked by pollsters for a formal estimate, the figure played back most often is the '10% gay' statistic which our propagandists have been drilling into their heads for years."[4]

Ten percent gay—nothing more than political *"propaganda"*? We've been down this same road before with the grossly inflated figures put forward for years by pro-abortion activists relative to the number of women who died from back-alley abortions before *Roe v. Wade*. When for a time it looked like the abortion clinics might be shut down by the Supreme Court, abortion activists, facing the possibility of having to go underground once again, began to admit how safe nonmedical abortions *had always been*!

In her chronicle of the landmark case which became the title of her book, *Roe v. Wade*, feminist Marian Faux revealed how statistical exaggeration on the part of pro-choice advocates was simply too effective to pass up:

> When I began to look into this aspect of abortion, several pro-choice reformers suggested that illegal abortion was not as dangerous as it had been depicted during the reform movement. Admittedly, an image of tens of thousands of women being maimed or killed

each year by illegal abortions was so persuasive a piece of propaganda that the movement
could be forgiven for its failure to doublecheck
the facts. The exaggeration was also a safe one.
Since these were illegal activities, no records
were kept, and the death and injury rate was
an impossible statistic to pin down.[5]

Instead of the 10,000 rumored deaths each year, the
figure was closer to 500. Dr. Bernard Nathanson, former
abortion reform activist and cofounder of the National
Association for the Repeal of Abortion Laws (and who
personally presided over 60,000 abortions), gives us this
interesting account of the deception practiced by the
abortion industry:

How many deaths were we talking about
when abortion was illegal? In N.A.R.A.L. we
generally emphasized the drama of the individual case, not the mass statistics, but when
we spoke of the latter it was always "5,000 to
10,000 deaths a year." I confess that I knew the
figures were totally false, and I suppose the
others did too if they stopped to think of it. But
in the "morality" of our revolution, it was a
useful figure, widely accepted, so why go out of
our way to correct it with honest statistics?

In pursuing the "morality" of their own gay revolution, do gay rights activists feel that the highly *useful* 10
percent figure is sufficiently compelling propaganda
that they can be forgiven for stretching the truth?

Apparently so. But at least some gay activists now
openly concede that they exploited the Kinsey estimate
for its tactical value, not its accuracy. "We used that
figure when most gay people were entirely hidden to try
to create an impression of our numerousness," says Tom

Stoddard, former head of the gay-oriented Lambda Legal Defense Fund.[6]

A concession by implication also comes from Tim McFeeley, executive director of the Human Rights Campaign Fund, a gay political-action committee. He warns fellow gay activists about the misuse of the Kinsey figure: "If you say a number that you can't prove, there's always the chance that, by disproving one part of your argument, your opponents weaken you overall. I think that's dangerous."[7]

Hopefully, this very chapter will demonstrate the validity of Mr. McFeeley's concern.

Enclave Perspectives

In a 1985 *Los Angeles Times* survey, more than half of those polled responded that they were not personally acquainted with *any* homosexuals—a fact which Kirk and Madsen dismiss by suggesting that straights simply weren't willing to admit there were any gays in *their* backyards. But why should that have been the case in the middle of the tolerant '80's? The issue is not whether any of us personally *know* people who are homosexuals. (As I indicated before, I myself know a number of gays.) The question is: Just how many practicing homosexuals in America are we talking about?

The truth is that most of us live in one kind of enclave or another. Gay activists on Fire Island could be excused for thinking that 30 percent of the general population was like themselves. Likewise, a large percentage of the population living outside major urban areas can legitimately say that they don't personally know *any* gays. That's especially true for Christians, who tend to isolate themselves within church circles and only interact with each other.

The enclave notion suggests that we need to be very careful about *how* and *where* polls are taken. What is the sample group being reported, and who is framing the questions? I found it highly interesting that in a footnote referencing the Kinsey study data, Kirk and Madsen added this significant tidbit:

> For a smaller, but more recent, survey that produced much the same results as Kinsey's, see M. G. Shively and J. P. DeCecco, "Sexual Orientation Survey of Students on the San Francisco State University Campus. . . ."

Are we to believe that the students at San Francisco State University represent a cross section of the general population? Given the claimed corresponding results, it would appear that Kinsey's reports are damned with faint praise!

Commenting on all the inflated statistics that have been coming our way about the gay population, London's *Sunday Times* reporter, Lynette Burrows, urges us to use our common sense as a backstop for what we hear from the "experts." Can it possibly be true that every tenth person we meet coming down the sidewalk is gay? "When it comes to judging the validity of what experts tell you, there is only one safe rule of thumb: a thing is either obvious, or it is obviously wrong."[8]

So How Many Gays Are There?

Now that the Kinsey study is being seen for the flawed report that it is, new studies are being done all over the world. In France (often cited by gays as having more liberal attitudes toward homosexuals), a 1992 survey found that only 4.1 percent of men and 2.6 of women report having had homosexual sex at least once in their lives. More significantly, only 1.1 percent of men and .03 percent of women had engaged in such activity in the previous 12 months.[9]

In Britain (where private acts of sodomy are exempted from criminal penalty) it is well-publicized that the

French believe all Englishmen are "puffs," as homosexuals are called. However, the most recent survey shows that the English are only slightly ahead of the French in that department. In 1987 the British Market Research Bureau carried out a detailed survey for the Department of Health and Social Services' "AIDS" unit. The survey found that only 1.5 percent of males could be described as active homosexuals. (The figure for bisexuals was 1 percent.)[10]

Back home in America, Judith Reisman, author of *Kinsey, Sex, and Fraud*, also puts the figure at 1 percent, while Paul Cameron's Washington-based Family Research Institute figure is closer to 3 percent. Connected as they are with more conservative leanings, these figures could be attacked as biased. But they correspond (even generously, in the case of FRI) with the figures just previously cited, and with what may be the most objective survey taken to date in the United States.[11]

For over 20 years the National Opinion Research Center, a polling group affiliated with the University of Chicago, has conducted the General Social Survey, related to a variety of social issues. NORC's director, Tom W. Smith, reports that between 1989 and 1992 two questions were added to its annual survey, which asked about sexual behavior.

The results have been consistent: Among men, 2.8 percent reported exclusively homosexual activity in the preceding year; among women, 2.5 percent. NORC is still tabulating the results of a full-scale, 3000-person sexual behavior study, but experts don't expect the numbers to be appreciatively different.[12]

As this book went to press, the latest figures emerged from the National Survey of Men, conducted by the Battelle Human Affairs Research Center in Seattle. Dr. John Billy reports that the 1993 survey revealed that 2.3 percent of all males had had "some homosexual contact" in the past ten years, but that only 1.1 percent had been exclusively homosexual in the previous year.[13]

What we are seeing, then, both home and abroad, is that the number of practicing homosexuals is ranging between 1 and 3 percent of the general population— nowhere near the mythical 10 percent. Even the gays are beginning to acknowledge this fact.

And why not? The 10-percent gay propaganda has served its purpose well. Now that the gays have political clout and have helped put their own man in the White House, there's no longer much need to play the deceptive numbers game.

Fatal Statistics

Perhaps the most macabre rebuttal to the "10 percent gay" propaganda lies in the silent coffins of the 100,000 gays who have died from AIDS since it was first reported in 1981. That's approximately 60 percent of the total 171,890 AIDS-related deaths reported as of December 1992 by the federal Centers for Disease Control and Prevention.[14] (Based on studies of transmission by the National Center for Health Statistics as of September 1991, 60 percent of the AIDs-related deaths resulted from homosexual or bisexual activity.)[15]

While gays themselves are the first to admit that AIDS has had a devastating impact on male homosexuals, that tragic statistic itself calls into question the size of the overall gay population. Some simple calculations will demonstrate what I mean.

Because female homosexuals are not affected as a particular class by AIDS, it is necessary first of all to take them out of the gay population group. Then, assuming that gay men outnumber their lesbian counterparts three to one (the estimate cited by pro-gay literature), the number of gay men in America—using the 10 percent figure—would be something over 15 million. Now we are set for the startling result. If there were really 15 million practicing male homosexuals in this country, the percentage among them of AIDS-related deaths would be no more than .007 percent!

Put differently, the chances of a male homosexual dying from AIDS would be something under one per thousand—a figure that gays would never even remotely accept. At .007 percent, we're talking about deaths from heart attacks (.006 percent by the national average)—not a dreaded plague! Reverse the process by which that figure was determined, and one can see that the number of active, practicing homosexuals in America is nowhere near the figures which have been claimed for so long.

How is one ever to tell the real statistics? Like their pro-abortion allies, gay activists have anonymity on their side. No one is able to keep accurate records of every homosexual act. But it is clear that there is absolutely no way that gay activists can justify the propagandist "10 percent."

In Search of Normalcy

The important question is, Why are the percentages and numbers so hotly contested? The answer is simple: *It is absolutely crucial for gays to portray homosexual behavior as normal. If it's normal, it's natural; and if it's natural,* how could it possibly be wrong? It's almost like saying that one out of every ten people is left-handed. Ten percent is a figure well within the range of normalcy. There's nothing freakish about being left-handed! Therefore, how could there be anything wrong with being left-handed *or gay*?

To further enhance their normalcy, gays love to point out that, at 10 percent, the practice of homosexuality is more commonplace than bowling (6 percent), jogging (7 percent), golfing (5 percent), hunting (6 percent), and so on. What are we being told here? That gay sex is just another recreation of choice? If so, should we expect to see bowlers, joggers, golfers, and hunters following suit to demand special minority legislation? Surely you've heard all the slurs that have been leveled against those polyester-clad suburbanites who frequent smoke-filled bowling alleys. . . .

The point, apparently, is that if you get enough people to do what you yourself do, then you'll *all* be morally right in whatever you're doing. No, it doesn't necessarily have to be a moral majority. In fact, for gay activists, anything *but* the moral majority is preferred!

All of this has interesting implications when you compare the probable 1-to-3 percent figure for gays with the 3 percent of the general population who have committed crimes against society, half of whom are currently in prison, or on parole or probation. Is the defense of crime-ophobia soon to be heard in courtrooms throughout the land? (With crime, at least the *phobia* part would be legitimate.)

Morality, of course, has absolutely nothing to do with statistics. I take it that gays would fully agree on at least one point—that no amount of Nazi consensus in Germany could justify Hitler's systematic slaughter of homosexuals in the Holocaust.

In the movement for gay rights, the numbers game works yet another way. If gays can con us into believing that they are as numerous as blacks and Hispanics, then they are halfway home in convincing us that they are a legitimate minority—not just a maladjusted individual here and there, but a "queer nation" within a nation.

Let's face it, there truly *is* strength in numbers—unless, of course, you just happen to be in that 40 percent of the general population who regularly assemble for worship. Naturally, that particular statistic instantly brands you as an oppressor, presumably seeking out every opportunity for bigoted actions against anyone who, by whatever personal choice, happens to be a 10-percenter or less. In such a case, the Constitutional right of free exercise explicitly guaranteed to the 40 percent becomes immediately suspect and vulnerable to abolition.

Did anyone ever say that the numbers game is played evenhandedly?

Gay Ranks Are Swelling

Of course, every successful fraud contains enough truth to make it believable. And the truth within the "10 percent gay" controversy is that there are indeed large numbers of practicing homosexuals among the general population, and plenty more who struggle with homosexual feelings without sexualizing them. And that number is growing every day—perhaps just because more and more closeted gays are "coming out," but perhaps also because there is less and less reason for those who are sitting on the fence *not* to act upon their feelings.

When Kirk and Madsen point to Kinsey's figures as coming *before* the sexual revolution of the '60's and '70's, they unwittingly point us to the real truth of the matter: Whatever might be the actual percentage of practicing homosexuals, *that percentage took a sizable jump during the two decades of unabashed sexual liberation.*

Based on that evidence, are we to believe that among the generation of Americans who became young adults in the swinging '60's there was an increased incidence of *genetic disorder* or *in utero dysfunction* leading to homosexual tendencies? Not likely.

What it tells us is that, contrary to vitriolic gay protestations, there is without a doubt a significant amount of personal choice in homosexual behavior! When sexual barriers fell in the free-spirited era of marijuana, hootenannies, and flower power, sexual activity of all types —both heterosexual and homosexual—took an upswing.

Homosexuals are in good company when they form alliances with pro-*choice* supporters. Theirs too is a lifestyle of *choice*. And the best evidence of that is how loudly they protest when they believe anyone is about to *take away* that choice!

That leads to a final observation. Whatever the actual figures for practicing homosexuals, it never has been nor ever will be as high as the figures for heterosexuals who engage in sex outside of marriage. Simply to make the point, let's assume that gays constitute 10 percent of the population, as they claim, and that same-gender sex was thereby considered "normal." Even so, they would be no more morally right than the 20 or 30 percent of *heterosexuals* who have sex outside the bonds of marriage.

When all is said and done, if gays constituted *99 percent* of the general population, their case for moral legitimacy would not be improved by even one percentage point. The morality of homosexual activity will always be as much a myth as the 10 percent gay statistic which gay propagandists have been drilling into our heads for years.

CHAPTER 5

The Confusing War of Words

Groups are subject to the truly magical power of words.

—Sigmund Freud

"Preference." "Lifestyle." "Gay." "Unnatural." "Perverted." "Sexual Orientation." "Homophobic." "Crime against nature."

The civil war over gay rights is not exactly a matter of semantics, but it comes close. One shudders at the thought of how much argument has been wasted because neither side understands *the words* the other side is using. On all sides, we have framed the issues so loosely (or cleverly) that we have little hope of understanding each other.

I'm not suggesting that some agreed-upon lexicon of terminology is going to win any debates or bring an end to the fighting, but perhaps we could be more clear-headed about where we agree and where we disagree. At least we would be playing on the same field.

A Stab at Clarity

May I suggest, first of all, that the term "homosexuality" is perhaps more neutral than most Christians have thought. On its face, "homosexuality" is *passive*. It refers to a state of being, or a condition. The idea is not of acting, but of being acted upon. Standing alone, it has no negative or immoral connotation. Unless one *insists* on assuming that the term includes actual sexual expression, then no Scripture condemns it.

If it helps you, consider "heterosexuality" in the same light. We know that one's heterosexuality can be sexually expressed in any number of ways that are sinful, but it is the expression itself—the *acts*—that are condemned, not one's heterosexuality. In fact, one's heterosexuality may never be acted upon in any manner. Even in today's sexually active society, there are still a good number of heterosexual virgins out there.

If that comparison still doesn't convince you, back up one more step to the root word that each term has in common: "sexuality." A dictionary definition of *sexuality* is: "the state or quality of being sexual." That should include just about everyone who has ever lived. It says nothing more than that we are biologically and anatomically equipped to engage in sexual relations and psychologically driven to express ourselves sexually.

So what do the terms "homosexuality" and "heterosexuality" say to us? They tell us about such things as orientation, proclivity, leanings, attractions, comfort zones, *dis*comfort zones. At some point fairly early in one's life everyone has—from whatever cause—a given sexuality, a personality or psyche or makeup that reflects either *hetero*sexuality (attraction for those of the opposite sex) or *homo*sexuality (attraction for those of the same sex). And, without more, there is little to be said about rightness or wrongness.

Certainly we could begin at this point to talk about what is "normal" and "abnormal," and look around demographically to see that *hetero*sexuality is "the norm." There has never been any dispute about this. *Normally*, a male has desires for those of "the fairer sex." And *normally*, a female is attracted to some strong man in her life.

If this means that homosexuality is "abnormal," all it

says for the moment is that we're counting heads. There are just a whole lot more people who identify with heterosexuality than homosexuality. But morally, we've hardly moved down the road. We're still pretty much in neutral territory.

Someone might point out that we could start getting into trouble when objects of *attraction* become objects of *lust*. Jesus himself told us that sin begins in the heart even before it is acted upon. And indeed somewhere along the line that becomes a concern, particularly for those whose fantasies begin to take over and control their minds. However, this would be true for heterosexuality as well as for homosexuality, and so, to that extent, it is less helpful than it might first appear.

What it does suggest is that, from a Christian perspective, it is often necessary to struggle with one's sexuality—that is, to keep from *acting* upon one's sexual urges. And that is just as true for those whose orientation is homosexual as for those whose orientation is heterosexual.

Given those parameters, the term *homosexuality* is used in this book in the neutral sense of "orientation." To say that it is neutral is not to say that it reflects God's intention for human sexuality. Because of its abnormality, homosexuality is an orientation that is most often characterized by a great amount of personal struggle. Whether because of social pressure from a mainly non-homosexual society, or simply because of inner turmoil reflecting the complex causes leading to its existence, it is not a comfortable orientation for most people.

That said, it is only when a person's homosexuality is *acted upon and sexually expressed* that we find ourselves in a different moral arena. When homosexual *behavior* occurs, we leave the relatively neutral territory of *orientation* and push our way deep into immorality.

What Is a Homosexual?

When we consider the words *homosexual* and *heterosexual* we face a frustrating inconsistency of usage. Despite their seemingly parallel meanings, the two terms can have quite opposite connotations. Like the word *heterosexual*, the word *homosexual* could abstractly mean nothing more than a person with that particular orientation. However, *always* in biblical usage and *typically* in social usage, the word *homosexual* connotes more than mere orientation. Its use assumes sexual practice, or an acting out of one's homosexuality. It moves from *status* to *conduct*.

If someone says of a man, "He's a homosexual," most of us automatically tend to assume that the man has engaged in homosexual sex. Whereas, if anyone ever bothered to say of another man, "He's a heterosexual," we might or might not think in terms of actual sexual relations. When we speak of heterosexuals, we generally tend to think only in terms of a person's orientation.

Undoubtedly, the reason for this subtle difference in usage lies in the distinction between what is normal and what is abnormal. Because heterosexuality is normal, one would hardly think to say, "He's a heterosexual." (So? Isn't everybody?) It's only when someone is *not* a heterosexual that we focus on the abnormality.

And how do we know that people are homosexual? By their *behavior*. By what they *do* sexually, not by their particular orientation (which, unless they tell us about it, is something we can never know).

I keep thinking how great it would be if we could clear away all the confusion by using some other word for those who are homosexually oriented, but who never sexualize their orientation. For men, how about the term *effeminate*? Close, but not good enough. Not all men who struggle with homosexuality are effeminate, and not all effeminate men struggle with homosexuality. (And what term do we possibly use for women who fall into this category?) It's all very complicated!

Because of the accepted connotations, both biblical and social, you will find the word *homosexual* used in this book only in reference to a person, male or female, who *actually engages in homosexual conduct*. Homosexual orientation *alone* does not mean that someone is a homosexual.

"Sexual Orientation": Deceptive Buzzwords

In the latest round of gay-rights activism, we're hearing a lot about the term "sexual orientation." It's in all the statutes and local ordinances prohibiting discrimination against gays. By all rights, "sexual orientation" is a neutral, passive term. That's why it works so well in the crusade for special legal protection. It's a word of status, like "black" or "gender." It's not something you do; it's something that happens to you.

But when gays wonder why there is so much uproar over their special-interest legislation, it's because they are cleverly *employing* the term one way but *meaning it* and *acting it out* another way. Yet despite the millions of people who fall for the slick advertising, not everyone is fooled by the linguistic "bait and switch," and they're the ones who are making such a fuss. And well they should!

If sexual *orientation* were the only issue, there never would *be* an issue. No one discriminates against other people on the basis of the particular sexual attractions a person might privately feel within himself. It bears repeating: Unless someone acts upon his orientation, or tells another person about it, there is no way that anyone would ever know. "For who among men knows the thoughts of a man except the man's spirit within him?"[1]

Those who oppose gay-rights legislation are not reacting in outrage to anyone's particular orientation, *but only to the insistence that one be given an unlimited moral right to express that orientation sexually*. That's even more than society is willing to give *heterosexuals!*

Note, for example, the age-of-consent laws; and prohibitions against adultery (still on the books in several states!) and, of course, prostitution. Note also the almost nonexistent legal status of heterosexuals who choose to live together without the benefit of marriage. Do gays really believe that it's just their own orientation that deprives them of society's good graces?

A person may not be able to change his or her homosexual orientation (status)—at least very easily—but it has yet to be demonstrated that there is no personal control over one's actions (conduct). It's no different from heterosexuals. Just because they are attracted to the opposite sex (status) doesn't give them free license in every situation to act upon that attraction (conduct).

When one *acts* upon his or her impulses, moral character comes into the picture. When one *expresses his or her sexuality*, invariably there are moral implications. At the point where gays depart from *orientation* and begin to demand acceptance of an aberrant *behavior*, society has every right to sit up and take notice. No man is a sexual island unto himself.

If you have any lingering doubts about the connection between the statutory language, "sexual orientation," and what gays are *really* after, consider this simple scenario. Just imagine what would happen if you were hauled into court and charged with illegal discrimination on the basis of "sexual orientation" for refusing to rent an apartment to a gay couple. If you defended by saying, "It was not their *sexual orientation* to which I objected, but only their *conduct*," you can bet that neither the gay couple nor their counsel—nor especially the judge—would be impressed with the nicety of that distinction! You would be summarily reminded that "sexual orientation" *includes* its sexual expression.

And it is that very assumption which Christians find objectionable. When gays say that they resent being defined solely by what they do in bed, it is the gay movement itself which is mandating that definition.

Make no mistake about it: It's not homosexual *orientation* for which gays seek legal protection, but homosexual *conduct*. It's not orientation alone which gays want to promote in America's classrooms as being socially acceptable, but homosexual behavior. Nor is orientation the issue at stake in the movement to gain legal recognition of homosexual marriages and adoptions. And if you take a close look at the criminal statutes that gays find so offensive, not one prohibits "homosexuality" or "orientation," just sodomy as the expression of this orientation.

Even though gays have astutely chosen to talk about "sexual orientation," we must never forget that what they really mean is "sexual behavior." And as long as it is "sexual behavior" which they wish to have publicly accepted, then they can hardly expect society to grant them legal protection for the "sexual orientation" behind which they hide their immoral conduct.

Responding to the way gays have fused together orientation and behavior, Christians correctly perceive that homosexuals *do* have choice, at least in terms of behavior and personal responsibility. At that point, of course, gays quickly and conveniently eliminate behavior from the equation, and speak only of orientation. "See, we really *don't* have any choice," they respond.

A Matter of Choice

This brings us to words of choice, such as *preference* and *lifestyle*. Like the trial lawyer who has no hesitation to argue two entirely inconsistent theories of defense as long as the jury brings in a verdict on either one of them, gays also seek our verdict on the basis of two clearly contradictory arguments.

In the normal flow of events, gays speak frankly of what they do in terms of sexual *conduct* (as when they wish to enjoy their supposed Constitutional freedom of sexual preference or lifestyle). In that context, the exercise of personal choice is freely and openly acknowledged.

But when, on the other hand, it is expedient for them to speak in terms of *status* (as when trying to obtain the rights of minority groups like race and gender), then the argument is made that homosexuals have no choice about who they are sexually.

At this point there is a sense in which both sides tend to lose their way, seeing the issue only in stark contrasts: Either that homosexuals have an orientation over which they have no control (like race and gender) or that they are engaged in conduct over which they quite obviously have personal control (in the same way as heterosexuals). In fact, the truth is closer to a combination of both statements.

We Christians need to realize that homosexuals usually have little choice about their *orientation*. As we will see in the next chapter, it is not genetic, as some argue; instead, for a complex variety of reasons (typically family-related) the orientation happens without anybody asking for it.

But gays themselves need to be honest enough to admit that they have personal choice over how to express their sexuality. Hiding behind the facade of their uninvited orientation in order to "celebrate the joy of homosexual love" should be beneath them. Nor is it worthy of them to suggest that it's somehow unchristian for us to acknowledge their orientation yet deny their moral right to act pursuant to that orientation. That argument is as bankrupt as a heterosexual saying, "Because I am heterosexual, I can have sex whenever and however I please!"

Is Homosexuality Natural?

That leaves us with the terms "natural" and "unnatural." And here we must be more perceptive than ever before. First, we must check to see whether we are talking about a *homosexual* as a sexually active individual or his *homosexuality*, his orientation. If the former, then we can say with complete confidence that it is not natural for two men or two women to have sex with each other. In acting out his or her sexuality, the homosexual is doing that which is "contrary to nature." More on this shortly.

On the other hand, if we are talking about a person's homosexual orientation, then its "naturalness" must be considered in two significantly different ways: 1) Is it, for whatever reason, "natural" for that individual? and 2) is it "natural" for *anyone* to be homosexually oriented?

The first question is more easily answered. If a person's sexual orientation is the "deeply ingrained frame of reference" which all of the evidence seems to suggest, then it is the only orientation that he or she will likely have known. Thus it is fair to say that one's sexual orientation is "natural" *for that individual.*

However, it remains to be seen whether what may be "natural" for the individual is "natural" on a different, more spiritual level, if you will. Is it in keeping with "the natural order"? Is it God's perfect will that any individual should be so oriented?

For a child who grows up in a home filled with hatred and abuse, child abuse could be said to be "natural" *for that child.* It may be all she has ever known. But no one would dare suggest that *child abuse itself* is "natural." That is the kind of distinction we are talking about with one's homosexual orientation: perhaps natural for the individual, but definitely not natural in the overall scheme of things.

It's Extremely Complicated

When we say to others that homosexuality is *unnatural*, and that its physical expression is *"a crime against nature,"* we need to clearly understand and articulate what we mean by those words. As always when it comes to sexuality (and sadly today, even love), we tend to focus immediately upon the sex act itself.

In the case of homosexuals, the first thing to project itself on the screens of our imagination is the image of two men engaged in anal sex. And of course that is a disgusting, repulsive image. How, we ask, could such an act *not* be unnatural!

But just because something is *disgusting* does not necessarily mean that it is *immoral*, or else what are we to say about human defecation? It has to be said that, although it conjures an image which we wouldn't want to dwell on, the elimination of human waste is a perfectly natural bodily function. What *can* be said, ironically, is that any sexual use of an orifice intended for human defecation is—by definition— *not* natural. (If that were ever in doubt, the medical evidence alone demonstrates what an unnatural assault on the body is made when the rectum is regularly employed as a substitute for what was intended to be the natural sexual organ.)

Disgust alone, however, is a poor determinant for what is morally wrong. Even with sexual acts, there are varying views among happily married heterosexual Christians as to what might be considered disgusting. For example, oral sex may be repulsive to some couples, even though many Christian couples today practice it.

Admittedly, whether or not Christian couples practice any given sexual act does not confer moral legitimacy on it. The point is that, in the reverse, neither does personal disgust alone make an act either unnatural or immoral. It is noteworthy that, with the possible exception of the prohibition against menstrual intercourse in the laws of Moses,[2] the Bible nowhere hints at the rightness or wrongness of particular types of sexual acts within a marriage relationship.

When it comes to revulsion at the thought of particular sexual acts, I remember being told the story of little six-year-old Julie, the daughter of close friends, and her reaction to a description of lovemaking. When she first asked her mommie about the birds and the bees she was given a simple, but completely frank, explanation of the act of intercourse. According to her mother, Julie's response was a mixture of disbelief and disgust.

As Julie's reaction reminds us, disgust may be in the eye of the beholder. Not so with morality, for true morality is always seen through the eyes of God. In his eyes, as revealed to us through biblical as well as natural revelation, homosexual conduct is unnatural—and therefore *morally* repugnant. Its *moral* repugnance has little to do with the actual form of coitus, and virtually everything to do with the fact that man is joined with man, or woman with woman.

Seen from a moral perspective, hugging, kissing, and holding hands by same-gender couples can be just as morally inappropriate as anal or oral sex. In fact, even nonsexual affairs of the heart between two men or two women would be "against nature." Sex aside, men are not meant to be romantic partners for men, nor women for women.

Clearly, we are not talking here about the close bonds of friendship that are often formed between two people of the same gender, which are not only unquestionably moral but also biblically encouraged. A good test of the difference between "close friendships" and "same-sex romantic interests" is whether the individuals involved also have healthy opposite-sex relations.

Creation Defines What Is Natural

When God said, "It is not good for the man to be alone. I will make a helper suitable for him,"[3] God did not create another man. Another man would not have been a suitable partner for Adam, any more than any one of the animals which God had previously paraded before him. That, incidentally, is why bestiality, just as homosexuality, is forbidden in the laws of Moses. It is not just the act of coitus with an animal that is so repulsive, but the unnaturalness of a human being having a relationship with a brute beast.

For that matter, fornication between heterosexuals suffers partly from the same problem. Outside of marriage, the act of sex is morally wrong because it is not integral to a committed love relationship. Little wonder that promiscuous sex of all types often bears such a resemblance to animalism!

Yet if it should be argued that committed love relationships between homosexuals can overcome these objections, then we're still missing the point. By God's creative mandate, genders are not interchangeable, whether for sex or for any other purpose. Despite what has become conventional wisdom (sadly even in the church), males and females are as different spiritually and psychologically as they are biologically.

Living in England for six months each year has taught me an important lesson about adaptability. Several American visitors have brought over 110-volt appliances, together with adapter plugs electrically unsuitable for British sockets. Time and again before I have a chance to warn them, I hear cries of distress when they successfully plug in an appliance only to find that they have just burned up a perfectly good curling iron or hair dryer!

The moral of the story is: You can plug into anything you want, but it won't necessarily work!

Worse than not working, homosexual behavior does to those who engage in it exactly what plugging into a 240-volt socket does to a 110-volt appliance. It destroys! Why? Because it was not designed for such a connection. It's an *unnatural* connection. It's *abnormal*. It's a *perversion* of intended function. Yes, it's *odd*. Even *queer*, in a proper use of the word. It was never meant to be.

Morality doesn't happen in a vacuum. God didn't just make up a long list of sins meant to provoke us and keep us from enjoying ourselves. To the contrary, the identifying of sin—*all sin*—is simply God's early-warning signal that we are about to do something that is not at all in our best interest. It's the danger sign on the curve ahead. It's the manufacturer's operating instructions printed in bold, capital letters: **WARNING ABOUT IMPROPER USE**.

That's what the "crime against nature" is all about. That's why homosexual relations are "unnatural" even if one's particular orientation is "natural" *for him*. The homosexuality which may be "natural" because it is the only orientation one has ever known is nevertheless "unnatural" when viewed in the perspective of God's intended creation. If one's natural sexual orientation is toward members of his or her same gender, then something has gone terribly wrong.

Chinese homosexuals have a hand signal that helps them identify one another. They hold their hands parallel and then flip them over quickly. It means, "I am inverted."[4]

I much prefer that to our term *perverted*, which has played too well into the hands of gay activists. When we talk about homosexuals being "perverts," it makes us look like we are merely hateful. If we want to convey more clearly the concern we genuinely have from a Christian perspective, we might give some thought to using the Chinese term.

In God's eyes, that's what homosexuals have become: sexually *inverted*.

Political Wordpower

If you wonder whether all this talk about terminology is really necessary, in my own judgment it is at the very heart of the matter. It should be obvious that gays are masters at the art of political wordpower. Look how successfully they have hijacked the word *gay* to replace the more repugnant sounding *homosexual*. And think what mileage they have gotten out of *homophobia*! With just two words, they have both given themselves respectability and effectively impugned those who would champion morality.

Of course, as Isaiah reminds us, it comes with the job, calling good evil and evil good:

> Woe to those who call evil good and good evil, who put darkness for light and light for darkness, who put bitter for sweet and sweet for bitter.[5]

Satan himself needed only a little three-letter word, "not,"[6] to introduce yet another three-letter word of enormous proportions, "sin."

In this book, the word *gay* is used in reference to practicing homosexuals who present themselves to be morally indifferent regarding their conduct and, more specifically, to political activists in the gay-rights movement. It is never used in reference to homosexuals who are struggling to do the right thing morally. They, of all people, know the difference between "gay" and "tragic."

CHAPTER 6

Can a Homosexual Change His Spots?

The natural man has only two primal passions, to get and beget.

—Science and Immortality

As Shirley MacLaine tells it in her book *Out On a Limb*, she has had many past lives. In some of her previous incarnations she was male, while in others, female. Or so says her psychic, Kevin Ryerson, and the astral plane entity, "John," whom he supposedly channels. Shirley's curiosity was aroused when "John" told her that everyone had experienced living as different sexes.

> "Could that be a metaphysical explanation for homosexuality?" [Shirley asked.] "I mean, maybe a soul makes a rocky transition from a female to a male body, for instance, and there is left over emotional residue and attraction from the previous incarnation?" "As such," said John, affirmatively.[1]

Well, that's certainly a novel explanation of the much-debated cause of homosexuality. But not one, I hope, that many people would seriously consider.

And then there's masturbation. It has its own advocates as the cause of same-sex attraction—sort of a variation on going blind, I suppose. But the advocates are deadly serious, as indicated by the classic (1886) explanation by Dr. Richard von Krafft-Ebing:

> If the youthful sinner at last comes to make
> an attempt at coitus, he is either disappointed
> because enjoyment is wanting . . . or he is lack-
> ing in the physical strength necessary to ac-
> complish the act [and this] leads to absolute
> psychical impotence. . . ."[2]

That sad state of affairs supposedly transforms the young man's sexual orientation into homosexuality, in which, presumably, he is able to overcome his "psychi-cal impotence" and regain the physical strength to have homosexual coitus!

As these two rather bizarre hypotheses alone indicate, the cause of one's sexual orientation has been the subject of heated controversy in books, scientific studies, and scholarly articles for as long as anyone can remember. Gather together a group composed of medical doctors, evangelists, psychiatrists, and gay activists to discuss this subject, and you can be assured of a real donny-brook!

The most widely discussed theories fall into two main categories, leading us back to familiar pairings that we've seen before in any number of controversies: *Born* or *bred*? *Nature* or *nurture*? *Heredity* or *environment*?

There are any number of permutations within these extremes, but a cursory look at each one will give us some idea of the latest thinking. One has to say even from the start that the very disarray witnessed among the experts must surely tell us something—probably that no single theory, standing alone, is the complete answer.

It also probably tells us that any profound social, legal, or moral implications that a person would wish to draw from any single theory should be immediately suspect. That is all the more true since the theories relate only to a person's sexual *orientation*, not to his or her sexual *behav-ior*. Until it is established that a person's sexual behavior is *mandated* by his or her orientation, then what might have caused the orientation is pretty much academic.

The same is true in other areas of social concern. We don't pretend to fully understand what causes a person to become a murderer or rapist, yet we don't hesitate to deal with his criminal behavior. Root causes often elude us. But we live in a real world where we choose (and are held responsible for) our behavior, despite any number of adverse circumstances, false starts, and twisted origins.

Didn't I Read About a Study Where...?

1991 was a banner year for the gay movement in terms of scientific research. Within just months of each other, two different studies by gay researchers hit the headlines as dramatic evidence that gayness begins in the chromosomes. The news sparked hopes that the findings might undercut the animosity that gays have contended with for centuries and lead to greater civil-rights protection. If, in fact, a genetically immutable characteristic responsible for homosexual orientation could be demonstrated, then there would be all sorts of wonderful implications for the gay movement.

Discovery of a "homosexual gene" would instantly take away any choice in the matter of orientation, and that in turn would mean (at least in the minds of gays) that homosexuals could no longer be imputed with moral guilt for their deviant behavior. It would also bolster the notion that gays are a "natural" minority, like race and gender—a crucial factor in gaining legal protection against discrimination. Finally, it would absolve guilt-ridden parents the world over of any fault in raising children who "went gay."[3]

Other, quite opposite implications, disturb even a fair number of gays. If homosexuality is found to be largely a biological phenomenon, then gayness starts to look less like a "preference" or "lifestyle," and more like an illness in need of a cure. And finding that cure resurrects chilling images of German doctors drilling into the skulls of homosexuals in search of the source of one's homosexuality.[4]

But what are we to make of the studies themselves? Are they intrinsically valid? In the first and most widely publicized study, Simon LeVay, a neuroscientist at the Salk Institute in La Jolla, California, put forward his findings that a specific area of the brain is smaller in homosexual males than in other males.

That tiny bit of gray matter, smaller than a snowflake and found in a bundle of neurons in the hypothalamus (which regulates heart rate, sleep, hunger, and sex drive) was nearly three times as large in the 16 heterosexual men studied as in the 19 homosexual men who were the subjects of LeVay's autopsies.

LeVay admitted that his research was far from conclusive. Because each of the homosexual men had died of AIDS-related causes, it could not be known whether the virus might have had some effect on the brain structure. And no women's brains were examined, whether from homosexuals or heterosexuals.[5]

Fellow Salk researcher Kenneth Klivington raises the inevitable chicken-and-egg question regarding the hypothalamus: Does its size determine homosexuality, or does homosexuality determine its size? "You could postulate," he says, "that brain change occurs throughout life, as a consequence of experience."[6] In other words, "Use it or lose it."

Frances Stevens, editor-in-chief of *Deneuve*, a lesbian news magazine, was also skeptical of the findings: "If the gay guy's [hypothalamus] is smaller, what's it like for dykes? Is it the same size as a straight male's?"[7] Good question.

The most serious broadside to LeVay's findings comes from gay activist Darrell Yates Rist, cofounder of the Gay and Lesbian Alliance Against Defamation, who believes that progressive gay researchers looking for evidence of genetic gayness undermine the dynamic of personally chosen sexual preference. Given what Rist describes as "nearly universal male-to-male lovemaking among citizen classes in some periods of ancient Greece and Rome," he asks, "would LeVay argue that all the great men of classic antiquity had an undersized hypothalamus?"[8]

The Sins of Twins

"Survey of Identical Twins Links Biological Factors with Being Gay," read the headlines. And the story flashed all across America. In the Archives of General Psychiatry, Northwestern's J. Michael Bailey and psychiatrist Richard C. Pillard of the Boston University School of Medicine had just reported new evidence that genetics play a more important role than environment in the development of homosexuality.

The evidence? Among 56 homosexual men who were twins, 52 percent of their identical-twin brothers were also homosexuals. By contrast, only 22 percent of *non*-twin brothers and only 11 percent of adoptive brothers were found to be gay.[9]

I love the way these findings were reported by Thomas H. Maugh II, science writer for the *Los Angeles Times*: "Identical twins have identical genetic makeups and, if homosexuality has a genetic basis, many of the second twins should also be gay. That is what they found: 52% of the identical twin brothers were gay."[10]

Am I missing something? If identical twins have *identical* genetic makeups, then why was the percentage of the second twins not *100* percent? Far from proving the *existence* of a genetic factor, the study is the best evidence yet of its *nonexistence*!

Surely what the 52 percent finding indicates is either that there is *no genetic factor at all* or that, even if there were, *a person's sexual behavior could be modified despite his orientation.*

What the study also appears to be telling us is that brothers tend to be influenced in similar ways within the same home environment. If there is a relational problem for one, it is likely (though not necessary) that it will be a problem for the other. If you take identical twins with remarkably similar personal makeups, then the likelihood of similar effects on sexual orientation could very well increase noticeably. That would easily account for the difference between the identical twins and the non-twin brothers.

And then there is the wonderfully profound conclusion drawn by Dean Heimer, molecular biologist for the National Institutes of Health: "If you think about it, there must be a strong genetic component to heterosexual orientation, or the species would not have survived so long. So it is only natural that there is a genetic component to homosexuality as well."

Some of the rest of us may not know as much about science as a molecular biologist, but, in all deference, doesn't simple logic pull us aside and ask a couple of pertinent questions here? First, if survival of the species dictates a heterosexual orientation (and he's undoubtedly right about this), then why does survival of the species permit the existence of a homosexual orientation? (I don't think gays are going to like any answer which implies that they are inferior, aberrant genetic mutations.)

More importantly, has Heimer never heard about environment thwarting nature's intent? Every twisted windblown tree shows how that can happen. Even when it comes to human behavior, we have never accepted the idea that deviant social orientation is necessarily genetic. The psychopathic killer is more likely to be the product of social environment than of any inherited genetic makeup.

Pillard himself recognizes the problem raised by Heimer's reasoning, even while attempting to sidestep it: "It seems to me that just because something is genetic or biological doesn't justify it clearly. If serial killers turned out to be genetically programmed we wouldn't say, Oh, well, it's OK."

But, of course, that's *exactly* what we say when we are convinced that someone's criminal act is the product of mental processes beyond his control. Certainly, we don't just turn him loose on society, but neither do we find him either morally or legally responsible. Is this really how gays wish to be regarded—not responsible for their actions by virtue of a genetic defect?

It is worth noting that studies are notoriously subject to being refuted by other, equally credible studies. For example, in 1992 the *British Journal of Psychiatry* reported the results of a study in which, of 46 homosexual men and women who were twins (both fraternal and identical), only 20 percent had a homosexual co-twin. The report concluded that "genetic factors are insufficient explanation of the development of sexual orientation."[11]

Until there is evidence which rises above the level of speculation, we must reject the notion that homosexuality is sheerly genetic. As one psychoanalyst puts it, the only solid *biological* evidence available is "that we're anatomically made to go in male-female pairs."[12]

Genetic Determinism?

The year 1993 brought yet another flurry of headlines proclaiming discovery of a gay gene. With great fanfare, National Cancer Institute researcher Dean Hamer announced that his team had isolated an area thought to lie somewhere along the X chromosome that a mother has contributed to her son. Contrary to the headlines, no "gay gene" had actually been discovered. It was still only a theory. But the press had already done its work in once again convincing a sound-and-sight-bite world that homosexual orientation is genetic.[13]

Hardly anyone was still listening, but Oxford geneticist Lawrence Russell immediately came forward to warn that "You can only identify what a gene does in company with other genes. Probably every gene is part of a multi-gene complex; there is not one single gene producing a single result."[14]

Speaking more broadly, distinguished Harvard University professor Ruth Hubbard, author of *Exploding the Gene Myth*, denounced the unwelcome trend she describes as "genetic determinism," a phenomenon she regards as owing more to a desire by some scientists to justify their narrowly focused genetic work—and the mega-dollars that fund it—than to good science. (Indeed, what does explain why *gay gene* research is being done at the National *Cancer* Institute?) Hubbard pointed to earlier heralded genetic "discoveries" pertaining to schizophrenia, manic-depression, and alcoholism—the later retractions of which have never gotten the same publicity as the so-called discovery.[15]

Oxford's Richard Dawkins, author of *The Selfish Gene*, agrees with Hubbard that "the body of genetic determinism needs to be laid to rest." Room doesn't permit Dawkins' rather complex explanation, but his conclusion is clear: "Whether you hate homosexuals or whether you love them, whether you want to lock them up or 'cure' them, your reasons had better have nothing to do with genes. Rather admit to prejudiced emotion than speciously drag genes in where they do not belong.[16]

View from the Psychiatrist's Couch

Until 1973, psychiatry was fairly unified in its understanding that homosexuality was a mental and emotional disorder. But bowing to the pressure of gestapo-type lobbying by gay activists,[17] the American

Psychiatric Association took homosexuality off the list of disorders and redefined it innocuously as "sexual orientation disturbance."[18]

In a 1974 referendum, 37 percent of APA members expressed their disapproval by voting against the redefinition.[19] However, only a year later their colleagues in the American Psychological Association recommended "removing the stigma of mental illness that has long been associated with homosexual orientation."[20]

At the mere mention of "mental illness," one begins to wonder if the gays weren't right to raise a fuss. "Mental illness" sounds a lot more like something *mental* than *emotional*. (Even more *genetic*?) I find it curious that most Christian writers on this subject lament the shift away from the "mental disorder" characterization. Is "mental disorder" consistent with the "free will" factor that is inherent within a Christian view of homosexual behavior?

To avoid the semantical battle and permit us to get to the heart of the matter, perhaps it is best simply to focus on the *treatment* of homosexuality, then and now. Before homosexuality was taken off the list of emotional disorders, psychiatrists and psychologists regarded it as (to use a neutral word) a "condition" in need of therapy. After the "condition" was redefined, the mental health community scuttled any attempts to "cure" homosexuality and concentrated instead on helping homosexuals feel more comfortable about themselves.

Formerly, treatment was pretty much like the old saw: "Doctor, it hurts when I do this." "Okay, so don't do it." The updated message from psychiatry is: "Just go ahead. It's not good for your self-esteem to suppress perfectly legitimate deep-seated urges." Unfortunately, the jury is still out on whether gays are any happier since modern messiahs have begun saying, "Go your way and sin if it makes you feel better about yourself."

The most damaging part of this kind of "treatment" is that it ignores altogether any underlying cause. It simply *assumes* the "condition" and moves blithely on from there. Perhaps that is a reaction to the formulistic Freudian explanation which tended to pigeonhole homosexuality as a set piece—weak father, dominant mother—and pretty much ignored other scenarios.

Freud may well have gone overboard, as he often did, but few people today will completely scorn the role played by parenting, upbringing, and home environment in the early formation of a person's homosexual orientation. In his excellent book *Desires in Conflict*, Christian counselor Joe Dallas presents a formidable case for the origin of homosexuality being *relational*.

Dallas begins by insisting that "there is no such thing as a 'typical' homosexual. There is no one reason people become homosexual."[21] That said, Dallas convincingly demonstrates that "homosexuality is a relational problem having its roots in some relational deficit between parent and child, or child and other children, or other people and himself."[22]

One of the most important points which Dallas makes —of particular interest to parents of children who struggle with homosexuality—is that the parent, in particular, may not be to blame. "Some actually had wonderful parents, while some were raised by tyrants. It was their *perception* of their early relationships, not necessarily the facts themselves, that generated a response."[23]

The perception factor may explain, for example, why siblings don't react the same way to the same parents. By way of comparison, consider the fact that only one out of several children in a family may get involved in drugs or criminal activity. Did the parents treat that child differently, or did he or she simply respond differently to the same treatment? Orientation is broader and more encompassing than merely sexual orientation. Nor is orientation of any type simple to understand.

What does all this have to do with sexual orientation? "Emotional needs can and do sometimes become sexualized," says Dallas. "If these children suffer gender-identity disturbances, for example, they will keenly feel the need for a strong, accepting male or female to identify with."[24]

Typically (though by no means universally), an adult homosexual's relationship with the parent of the same sex was unsatisfactory. If he or she feels unacceptable to the same-sex parent, he or she may feel unacceptable to all members of the same sex. All it takes is for someone from the same sex to offer much-longed-for acceptance, and, all of a sudden, deep-seated sexual and emotional needs can dangerously intersect. If they do, *orientation* becomes *behavior*; *homosexuality* becomes *homosexual*.

Sissies and Tomboys—Embryonic Gays?

Before we race ahead to behavior and leave orientation behind, we simply have to deal with the typical image of the adolescent who seems to have a wrongly focused orientation. Admittedly, the image may be stereotypical, but few stereotypes exist without some basis in fact. Who better to tell us about it than gay researcher Simon LeVay, who says of himself (and of his homosexual brother), "When I look back, I definitely see things that went along with being gay: not liking rough sports, preferring reading, being very close with my mother." And the clincher: "I hated my father as long as I can remember."[25] (Freud would certainly feel vindicated at *this* picture!)

But LeVay raises yet another extremely interesting chicken-and-egg question: Does the father's *perceived* rejection ("I don't love you!") cause his son to hide behind his mother's skirts and take on the softness of more feminine traits? Or, quite the reverse, does the son's perceived softness cause his father to reject him? ("This sissy can't be *my* son!")

I've got to believe that LeVay is onto something here, although not exactly the simplistic explanation that his hypothalamus theory would propose. Surely relational difficulties between parent and child, some of which are not even actual but merely perceived, cannot account for the *physical* characteristics so often associated with homosexual orientation.

Whence the classic lisp and the limp wrists? Whence the "pretty face with the rosy cheeks" that make the other boys taunt the playground sissy? Whence the decidedly masculine features of the girl who would rather roughhouse with the boys than sit demurely with her more feminine classmates? Are we to believe that *physical characteristics* are merely relational?

Or even *personality*? What makes one boy (or one brother?) strong and aggressive while another is weak and gentle? Who can trace the gossamer line between nature and nurture, biology and psychology?

We simply can't know all the subtle factors which may influence one's sexual orientation. If relational problems carry the most weight, as they seem to, even those are complicated beyond belief.

Is It Possible to Change?

I don't know for sure, but I suspect that anyone who has ever struggled with homosexual feelings might say at this point, "I know, better than you do, how unnatural and self-destructive my homosexuality is. And I fully appreciate how God's plan for human sexuality is *supposed to work*. But, try as I might, I'm just not heterosexually oriented. I don't have romantic feelings for members of the opposite sex; and, if you've ever struggled with heterosexual lust, that's exactly what it's like for me, only directed toward those of my own gender. What am I supposed to do?"

What I have given you is a more personalized version of one of the most crucial arguments put forth by the gay movement. It is claimed that the supposed inability to change sexual orientation is proof that homosexuals are discriminated against on the basis of a status over which they have no control.

These arguments squarely raise the issue of change. What is the truth of the matter? Can a homosexual change his spots?

From what we have already seen, the answer is *perhaps not*—at least not his "spots." Homosexual orientation comes about through an exceedingly complex combination of factors which are deeply ingrained in a person's psyche. But even so, there is overwhelming evidence that homosexuals can in fact change how they *respond* to their "spots." That is to say, homosexuals need not *act* pursuant to their orientation, any more than their heterosexual counterparts who, outside of marriage, must exercise a disciplined response to their own kind of "spots."

At some point, *orientation* may indeed be very difficult to change. (Difficult but not impossible.) *Conduct*, however, is always in our own hands.

Any other position forces us to a conclusion which I dare say few, if any, gays are willing to acknowledge: that homosexuals lack free will.

No matter how close the gay movement comes to making that very acknowledgement when they argue, "We can't help who we are," I don't know a single one of them who is eager to relegate himself to the status of a robot, programmed without personal choice to perform aberrationally moment by moment.

As a criminal law professor, I can't help but think of the obvious parallel when it comes to a discussion about personal responsibility. In criminal law, when a person claims that he or she knows the nature and wrongfulness of the act he is performing, but cannot conform his conduct to that which he knows to be right, he is usually claiming the defense of insanity.

Although the insanity defense requires a showing that the claimed volitional impairment is the result of mental disease or defect—something gays vehemently deny in their own case—the "gay-by-nature" argument is founded upon basically the same assumption: "It's beyond our control."

Is it, therefore, *insanity* to which gays are admitting when they claim freedom from personal responsibility for their homosexual conduct? Not likely.

And if insanity is "not likely," then only the opposite can be true—that homosexuals *can in fact* control their conduct if they choose to. It may not be *easy*, but that is not the issue.

When was personal conduct ever easy for anyone? Just ask the kid who grows up in the ghetto where gang participation is expected by his peers. Or the accountant who could pay off his wife's catastrophic hospital bills simply by dipping into company funds. Or, more to the point, the single Christian who is committed to sexual purity in the midst of a sex-saturated culture. Doing what is right is often far from easy.

For the homosexual, it may be more difficult still. Difficult, but not impossible. Difficult, but necessary. Difficult, but ultimately to one's greater happiness.

Scripture Says Change Is Possible

It may not speak very loudly to those who don't take the Bible seriously, but for those of us who do, something found in Paul's first letter to the Corinthians fairly shouts from the housetop regarding the change possible in homosexual conduct.

Look at this list of sins that threaten to keep us from entering into the kingdom of God:

> Do you not know that the wicked will not inherit the kingdom of God? Do not be deceived: Neither the sexually immoral nor idolaters nor adulterers nor male prostitutes nor

> homosexual offenders nor thieves nor the greedy nor drunkards nor slanderers nor swindlers will inherit the kingdom of God.[26]

Right off the bat, it is obvious that homosexual conduct, like heterosexual immorality, is assumed to be volitional—that is, it's something we can choose either to do or not to do. Otherwise, how could God possibly condemn it? How could we be kept from the kingdom of God if we are helpless and inherently unable to mold our lives in conformity with God's righteousness?

All sins assume personal responsibility. Homosexual sin is no exception.

But the clincher as far as the issue of *change* is concerned is found in the following verse:

> And that is what some of you were. But you were washed, you were sanctified, you were justified in the name of the Lord Jesus Christ and by the Spirit of our God.[27]

Did you catch the clincher? "And that is what some of you *were!*" "Some of you," says Paul, "*used to be* thieves, drunkards, swindlers, and homosexual offenders." That's what they *were*, but *now* they have been washed, sanctified, and justified in the name of Christ!

Lest anyone think that these thieves, drunkards, swindlers, and homosexual offenders were politely forgiven and then permitted to continue in their former lifestyle, Paul pointedly disabuses us of any such notion: "Do you not know that the wicked will not inherit the kingdom of God?"[28]

Lest anyone get the idea that Paul is unaware of the ongoing struggle that haunts those whose sinful lifestyles have become deeply ingrained patterns, that notion too is exploded in the very next verse: "I will not be *mastered* by anything."[29]

For Paul, it is a question of masters. Through revelation, the Master of the universe is telling us that, by his grace, homosexuals *can* master their abnormal sexual urges, at least to the extent of changing patterns of behavior.

Therapy Joins with Scripture

Should one prefer a more secular "master," there is the assessment by William H. Masters, the widely recognized sex therapist. Masters and his partner Johnson confirm scientifically that, not only can homosexuals master their urges to sexually express their homosexuality, but they can even find fulfillment in heterosexual relations.

What is significant about their report is that Masters and Johnson do not approach the issue from a moral or spiritual bias. They personally find nothing inherently wrong with homosexuality. In fact, says Masters, "we consider homosexuality a natural form of sexual expression. Mind you, we didn't use the word 'normal,' we said 'natural.'"

Disagree with him as we might on the questionable use of the term "natural," his findings confirm what the apostle Paul taught about the possibility of change. Stronger spiritual forces aside, even therapy can assist a male homosexual in changing to a vaginal orientation for his sexual expression.

The Masters and Johnson Clinic in St. Louis has treated hundreds of homosexuals and bisexuals. Masters reports that they have successfully "changed" more than half of their homosexual clients, and higher than 75 percent of bisexuals.

Testimonies to Change

I can tell you anecdotally and personally of a phone call I'll never forget from a former student who used to attend my Wednesday night Bible study, telling me excitedly of his eventual triumph after years of trying to free himself of enslavement to a homosexual lifestyle. Does this mean that he no longer fights the passions which once overwhelmed him? No. He is an ex-homosexual in *practice*, not in orientation.

I have painfully witnessed the roller-coaster progress of another young man who is very close to my heart, and rejoiced with him as he broke free from the chains of the gay culture in which he had been confined for years. Is his battle over? No. In fact, as with all who struggle with homosexuality, the battle almost never ends. But he has given up the homosexual lifestyle in which he was actively engaged and has committed himself to helping others do the same.

Multiply these two young men by scores of men and women in Christian support groups all over the country, and the "inability-to-change" argument is blown away. That's what such organizations as Homosexuals Anonymous, Love in Action, White Stone Ministries, Exodus, and Desert Stream are all about—*change*!

For anyone truly interested in the truth about homosexuals who have given up their former lifestyle and have committed themselves to sexual purity, the testimonies abound! Homosexuals not only *can* change how they respond to their abnormal sexuality, but by the grace of God they *do* change! And, of course, that fact is fatal to the argument that gays are like any other minority when it comes to civil rights. Who ever heard of a black person becoming white!

As *Newsweek* recently reported, "Perhaps the most voluble spokesman for the 'fix it' school is Charles Socarides, a New York City analyst who claims a flourishing practice in turning troubled homosexuals into 'happy, fulfilled heterosexuals'":

> He "reconstructs" patients' lives to learn why they can't mate with opposite-sex partners. There can be many reasons, he says:

"abdicating fathers, difficult wives, marital disruptions." From there, he "opens up the path" to hetero happiness, for which, he says, one gratified customer cabled him recently: "The eagle has landed."[30]

In light of such success among those who desire to do something about their homosexual lifestyles, this observation from psychologist Joseph Nicolosi, author of *Reparative Therapy of Male Homosexuality*, appears more and more ominous: "Psychology and psychiatry have abandoned a whole population of people who feel dissatisfied with homosexuality."

It's a rerun of another era, reported not by *Newsweek* and *Time* but by Jeremiah the prophet:

> "From the least to the greatest, all are greedy for gain; prophets and priests alike, all practice deceit.
>
> They dress the wound of my people as though it were not serious. 'Peace, peace,' they say, when there is no peace.
>
> Are they ashamed of their loathsome conduct? No, they have no shame at all; they do not even know how to blush. So they will fall among the fallen; they will be brought down when I punish them," says the LORD.[31]

As therapists Nicolosi and Socarides demonstrate, it doesn't take a Christian counselor to recognize that false starts with homosexuality can end up in victory! What it will take on a grand scale is a mental-health community that is willing to quit pandering to gay activists and get on with the compassionate job of helping homosexuals who hurt because they have been encouraged on every hand to freely and proudly express forbidden, if uninvited, desires.

CHAPTER 7

Lesbians and Playboys: Disoriented Sex

The birds and the bees are doing it,
Lesbians, even Lebanese are doing it,
Guys in heels and silk chamois are doing it.
                                        —Not Cole Porter[1]

To this point we have assumed a connection between orientation and behavior whenever there is homosexual conduct. But in a number of circumstances, no one even pretends that such a connection exists.

One illustration of this phenomenon is what is sometimes known as "institutional homosexuality." It refers to homosexual conduct which takes place, for example, among prisoners and sailors. In such cases the absence of a heterosexual outlet prompts some men, who otherwise would never consider it an option, to engage in same-gender sex. It has nothing to do with some deeply ingrained homosexual orientation—just sex, with whomever it might be available.

The possibility of this kind of homosexual behavior where individual orientation is not a factor is one of many considerations behind the military's objection to having gays in its forces. The last thing the military needs is any catalyst to get things going in the wrong direction. The potential for "institutional homosexuality" may explain why the Navy turns a blind eye to the welcoming arms of local prostitutes (and hands out condoms) when it docks for shore leave.

Lesbian Feminists or Feminist Lesbians?

Lost in all the rhetoric over the cause, or causes, of homosexuality is the response from a significant segment of homosexuals in America: lesbians. While lesbians too can be the products of relational beginnings (first innocently internalized, then volitionally sexualized), for many lesbians sexual orientation has little to do with their gayness. For them, gayness is just an extension of feminism—usually *radical* feminism. For them, being gay is just another way of saying, "We reject men."

As *Newsweek* reported, "Many of them say their choice of lesbianism was as much a feminist statement as a sexual one, so the fuss over origins doesn't interest them."[2] As one lesbian activist said of the nature/nurture debate: "It's mostly fascinating to heteros."[3]

Commenting on the fact that studies on the origins of homosexuality rarely give much ink to lesbians, Penny Perkins, public-education coordinator for Lambda Legal Defense and Education Fund (which promotes lesbian and gay men's rights) says, "It's part of the society's intrinsic sexism."[4]

Among lesbians, as indeed among a growing number of gay men, there is a noted disdain for any talk about the origins of homosexuality. For most gays, it simply doesn't matter. John DeCecco, professor of psychology at San Francisco State University and editor of the *Journal of Homosexuality*, found this out when he began one of his classes by suggesting that his students discuss the causes of homosexuality. When someone in the back of the room called out, "Who cares?" the class burst into uproarious applause![5]

Why do they not care? New York lesbian psychotherapist April Martin tells us straight out: "It has nothing to do with whether we were born this way or whether we evolved into our own creation. It has to do with the fact that it is morally wrong to oppress people based on

characteristics or behavior which cause no harm to anything except the established social hierarchy."[6]

In short, what most lesbians and gay men are saying
is, We *want* to do what we are doing, it causes nobody
any harm, and it's none of your business why we do it!
It's not a question of *origins* but *rights*. Says Martin, "The
question of whether homosexuals should have full legal
rights and civil rights and social acceptance [has] nothing whatsoever to do with whether we can or can't help
or change our inclination."[7]

A Trip to "Lesbianville"

For a fascinating (and altogether disturbing) collage of
images mixing lesbianism and radical feminism, one
need only visit the Pioneer Valley of Western Massachusetts and the community of Northampton, which
has become a mecca for feminist lesbians. There are
some 10,000 lesbians in the area (one-eighth of the
region's population), and half of Northampton's businesses are owned by women. One of those businesses, a
lingerie store called Gazebo, has abandoned its Gentleman's Night for Lesbians' Night.[8]

Among other same-sex announcements, the local
newspaper recently ran its first lesbian engagement
announcement. (Beth Grace and Karen Bellavance wore
matching earrings, which they gave each other on the
day "they" proposed.) Unitarian minister Victoria Saf-
ford said that since 1987 "the number of women asking
her to officiate at lesbian 'services of union' has increased
steadily."[9]

Many local residents refer to their community as "Les-
bianville." Some go so far as to call Northampton a kind
of lesbian Ellis Island: "All lesbians pass through here at
least once," so it is said.[10]

According to Richard Pini, owner of Northampton's
Pleasant Street Theatre, the influx in lesbian residents

was tied to nearby universities, including Amherst, and the two all-women institutions, Smith College and Mt. Holyoke College.[11] Graduates of Smith College include an interesting mixture of Nancy Reagan and Barbara Bush along with Betty Friedan, Julia Child, and Gloria Steinem. One gets the idea that some of the distinguished alumnae would not be terribly pleased with the feminist/lesbian flavors currently being served up at their alma maters.

Under growing pressure to disassociate Smith from the so-called lesbian connection, the administration at Smith College has recently gone to great lengths to play up their role as a legitimate women's institute of higher education, while playing down any idea that it is a recruitment center for lesbians.[12]

Certainly there is no necessary connection. Both radical feminism and lesbianism are alive and well on co-ed campuses all across the nation. It's just that, even in the story of one small community, there is the nagging hint that the ties between women's liberation and gay liberation are close indeed. Explaining the influx of lesbians into Northampton, Richard Pini noted, "This was also the era when the region's schools began to expand programs such as women's studies."[13]

Revealing Insights into Lesbian Thinking

One of the most outspoken reference works exploring the feminist/lesbian connection is the feminist handbook, *(The New) Our Bodies, Ourselves*, a publication arising out of the Boston Women's Health Book Collective. (The introduction to my British edition says of its co-editors, "Both writers have been actively involved in the Women's Liberation Movement for many years.)[14]

Under the heading "Fear of Lesbians and Our Unity As Women," the authors say that "some women hesitate to join feminist projects because friends and family assume that being a feminist means one is a lesbian. Ultra-conservative political and religious groups play on these fears by portraying all feminists as man-haters and actual or would-be lesbians."[15]

Certainly one wouldn't want to fall into the trap of lumping all lesbians into the same feminist mold. But even the authors recognize that "on the other hand, some lesbians struggling for legitimacy and acceptance suggest that 'straight' women are less feminist than lesbians or that 'true' feminists wouldn't ally themselves with men in any way."[16]

And from there the authors proceed to sprinkle throughout their book the following statements, which certainly *look* as if there is some man-hating reason for women to "turn lesbian":

> Each of us who loves another woman has grown up in a sexist society which devalues women and fails to give us a strong sense of identity.[17]
>
> Butch-femme relationships can become dangerously close to perpetuating sexism and oppressive heterosexual models.[18]
>
> As lesbians we have a chance to move away from male-defined sexuality.[19]
>
> When I'm having troubles with a man and tell a lesbian friend, she usually gets a look in her eye which means, "What did you expect, being with a man?"[20]

I find it interesting that a feminist can *become* a lesbian, or *deem herself* to be a "lesbian" even before sexualizing it:

> Our need for support and solidarity can be problematic in other ways too. Sometimes women "become" lesbian, and become part of a mutual support network, only to return later to a man.[21]

> I felt a strong political and personal commit-
> ment to women and a fascination for lesbians,
> but it scared me to think that maybe I wanted
> to love a woman—my parents would explode,
> my ex-husband would try to get custody of our
> kids, my friends might think I was out to
> seduce them. I was also afraid it would be a
> choice against men instead of for women.
>
> Slowly I worked through all this and finally
> one day I said to myself, "For now, I am a
> lesbian," and some important piece of my
> identity clicked into place. I'm glad I chose to
> be a lesbian before I had a woman lover.[22]

The matter of personal choice is also affirmed by the slogan "Every woman can be a lesbian," which appears on badges worn by members of the Gay Liberation Front. Even the National Organization for Women gets in on the act, saying, "The simple fact is that every woman must be willing to be identified as a lesbian to be fully feminist."[23]

In all of this, the question is whether lesbianism breeds feminism, or feminism breeds lesbianism. Or, indeed, whether lesbianism and feminism are paired sexual/political manifestations arising out of the same cauldron of relational origins. But who can doubt that there is a connection somewhere along the way?

"Man hatred" or no "man hatred," my guess is that, for lesbians and radical feminists alike, some serious mistreatment by a man somewhere along the way is always lurking in the background. It would not be surprising if male rejection, both politically and sexually, followed on the heels of such abuse.

There is no question but that, for the most part, lesbianism *as such* has the same basic origins as homosexuality for gay men—something deeply ingrained in the psyche, probably of a relational nature happening during the formative years. But the sexual expression of radical feminist political convictions is also well worth considering.

Unlike the middle-ground blending of genders which takes place with heterosexual expression, in both lesbianism and radical feminism there is a Balkanization of genders at the extreme. Ironically, once you emasculate gender differences, you invite antagonism rather than harmony. Perhaps that explains the acrid bitterness which characterizes much of radical feminism and lesbianism.

To the extent that lesbian behavior is politically motivated or associated, wholly apart from homosexual orientation, the call for gay rights among women is compromised. Under such circumstances, gayness as a *choice* is clear. And any talk about being a *natural minority* goes right out the window.

From More to Different

Shift with me now, if you will, back to primarily *male* homosexual behavior. A couple of years ago, a compelling BBC television documentary took the viewer to the fleshpots of Bangkok, Thailand, for an exposé of the prostitution industry, which, until the AIDS scare recently prompted the government to crack down on it, was wide open for business. It was the usual parade of girlie bars, peep shows, and massage parlors, until the cameras focused on two separate, more unusual aspects of the red light district.

The first quite-intended social commentary was underlined when a 12-year-old "virgin" was supplied for sex at the request of an undercover BBC journalist. As an obviously apprehensive young girl (sold into prostitution by her family from a poor region of the country) entered the hotel room, the journalist revealed to her pimps his identity and purpose. Naturally, they did a fast exit!

But the journalist had made his point. Even sex with an innocent child is available if you have the money in Bangkok. And apparently there was enough demand for underaged sex that a ready supply of young girls was always available.

The second social commentary might have been unintended, but was certainly suggested when BBC cameras entered a bar known as "The Orgy." This bar was not only a "girlie bar" but a "rent-boy bar" as well. The idea was not simply girls available for heterosexuals and young men for homosexuals, but everybody for everybody—including other customers if they so desired! According to the reporter, it was all-out, no-holds-barred sex by the hour. Whoever and whatever.

Upon reflection, one could see a connection between the two vividly portrayed scenes. Libertine sex, like alcohol and drugs, has a way of numbing the senses so that there's never enough of it. (If one prostitute gives a thrill, then two at a time must be better.) After awhile, even *more* is not enough. *More* must be escalated to *different*. And that's where the 12-year-old walks in. She's something different. *Very* different.

Of course, to be *different* it needn't be sex with underaged girls. It can simply be kinky sex.

After awhile, when even bizarre sex cannot satiate the sexual senses, where does the heterosexual male go from there? The possible answer is whatever turns out to be the local equivalent of The Orgy in Bangkok with its promise of sexual thrills yet to be experienced—even with someone of the same sex, if you get drunk enough first!

Don't forget what we are talking about in this chapter: homosexual behavior totally unrelated to homosexual orientation. It may not be a matter of being *persuaded*, merely *jaded*.

When the Bunnies Get Too Tame

I must admit that I struggled for a long time with whether I could present a sufficiently believable scenario to sell the idea of progressive heterosexual sex lapping over at some point into homosexual sex.

What first came to mind was the book entitled *Child-Loving* that is receiving so much press these days. Its author, James Kincaid, is a professor of English at the University of Southern California. In his book he passionately defends pedophilia—not that he recommends the practice nor admits to participating personally. Yet Kincaid seriously calls us to reassess our view of "kindly, rational people" who only want "to kiss, touch, tickle and treat the child as a 'cuddle bunny.'"[24] The fact that such a book is receiving rave reviews from American academics is certainly a telling commentary on our times. It makes me feel even more concerned for the little 12-year-old in Bangkok.

But I realized that even this unwelcomed concession to pedophilia was scant evidence of the progression I wanted to demonstrate. Frustrated, I went to the front door and picked up the morning paper. There, at the bottom of the front page, was exactly what I was looking for! The headline read: "Playboy chief admits to being bisexual."

In case you missed the report, *Playboy's* creator, Hugh Hefner, has "come out," acknowledging that he was a bisexual in the 1970's. According to Charles Laurence, reporting from New York:

> The founder of the Playboy magazine and clubs, and self-styled Father of the Sexual Revolution, said: "I was exploring the outer limits of my own sexuality and it included bisexuality."

Bunnies and Playmates spread themselves

over his glossy color pages, and staffed his nightclubs. They also hopped in and out of his fabled "console" bed, fitted with everything from drink coolers to television screens.

But his image of the man who had everything was based on the premise that what he had was young, blonde, bronzed, leggy—and, of course, female.

Now he tells *Details* that he agrees with Freud—the father, surely, of sexual neuroses —that all men are born bisexual.

But his former followers will be relieved to hear that he discovered at the outer limits of his sexuality that he preferred girls.[25]

Sigmund Freud's research is not the explanation for Hefner's bisexual behavior. Hefner's own highly touted "Playboy philosophy" is the true explanation. That philosophy is called "saturation sex." Or "sex for the sexually bored." When *more* gives way to *different*, no law says *different* has to be with the same sex!

And here, in Hefner's own words, is the revealing centerfold of the matter:

"I never really had an emotional connection with a man," he said.

All his romantic fantasies—the imaginings that inspired an era—were heterosexual.[26]

There we have it, from the man who ought to know. Homosexual *behavior* need not have anything to do with homosexual *orientation*. Hefner was not struggling with some innate homosexuality, or acting out some genetic impulse beyond his control, or sexualizing some deeply ingrained emotional need arising out of an unhealthy relationship with his father. He was simply *experimenting with sex*.

Ever since the sexual revolution of the sixties and seventies—fanned in large measure by Hefner's Playboy empire—sex has known few limits. The promise of promiscuous sex was socially accepted, legally condoned, and safeguarded by the pill. As for the burgeoning gay population, others may be convinced that it merely reflects the large number of homosexuals who have come out of the closet thanks to the freedom of the times. Personally, I suspect that there has also been a multitude of jaded, sex-saturated heterosexuals who have gone *into* the closet looking for more erotic skeletons to play with! After awhile, you can grow tired even of a room full of perfectly good toys.

And, of course, "toys" is the right word for "playmates." When America decided to separate body from spirit in order to facilitate the *more* of sex, it headed down a path that dehumanized sex altogether. It wasn't the *person* or *relationship* that mattered, only *bodies*. Only *genitals*. And when that became the highest goal of sex, then *any* genitals would do. After all, it was the "swinging 70's." We were only playing around.

If I'm anywhere near right in saying that homosexual behavior is not necessarily linked to orientation, then, in terms of alleged social, legal, and moral justifications, gay rights are in real trouble.

Not only that, but in light of the evidence pointing to homosexual experimentation by liberated heterosexuals, society also has every right to ensure that its young people are not encouraged in any way to follow in Hefner's shoes to "explore the outer limits of their sexuality." Particularly is that true of those young people whose fragile sexual orientation is already leaning in the wrong direction, just waiting to be sexualized if given the slightest encouragement. (That alone is reason enough to keep gays from having equal time in the classroom.)

Anthropology Needs No Apology

As Americans, we tend to suffer from cultural myopia. From our narrow peephole of time and place, we just naturally assume that "we *are* the world. We *are* the people." What others do around the globe hardly seems to matter. What others have done throughout history is irrelevant. But getting out of our cultural smugness and looking around a bit can be an eye-opener.

What does it tell us, for example, when we read the findings of anthropologists like Margaret Mead and Tobias Schneebaum, who have uncovered various tribes here and there with almost ubiquitous homosexual behavior? Are we to understand that everyone in the tribe had a smaller-than-normal hypothalamus? That *all* pregnancies somehow affected hormonal balance in such a way that every person in the tribe came out of the womb gay? Or even that *everyone in the tribe* experienced some relational deficit resulting in deeply ingrained homosexual orientation?

All of the same questions can be asked of ancient Greece and Rome, since every gay activist knows how widespread homosexual behavior was in those (now eclipsed!) civilizations. And need we ask the obvious question: What about the genetically determined "10 percent gay"? How are we to explain that bit of propaganda in light of cultures that supposedly are, or were, 50 to 90 perent gay?

The only answer in every case is that *orientation is only a small part of the equation*. Whatever a person's sexual orientation, and from whatever origins, when it comes to homosexual behavior, *cultural influences* tell the real story. Cultural influences act either as *fences* or as *gates*. They either *encourage* or *discourage* the lust for aberrant behavior.

And when we speak of "cultural influences," we're not necessarily talking about a *religious* or a *politically conservative* culture. It's not just Pat Robertson, Dan Quayle, and Pat Buchanan taking gratuitous shots at homosexuals, as gays suppose. Think again of the former Soviet bloc countries with their official atheist (*and* antihomosexual) policies. And you can add China to that list as well.

Homosexual practices have a long tradition in dynastic China. Emperors dating back thousands of years had their court "favorites." But under Chairman Mao Tsetung, homosexuality became a symptom of foreign imperialism. Even today, because it directly contradicts Maoist teachings that the purpose of sex is procreation and that anything more drains people of energy needed to rebuild Chinese society, homosexuality remains something that few Chinese accept or understand.[27]

Did you catch that phrase: "*Maoist teaching that the purpose of sex is procreation*"? Does this mean ACT-UP is going to march into the Great Hall and disrupt the proceedings there like they interrupted the mass at St. Patrick's Cathedral during the infamous "Stop the Church" protest? Is it even remotely possible for gays to understand that it's not just the Pope and fundamentalist Christians who find homosexual behavior objectionable?

From history, sociology, and anthropology, what we learn is 1) that it's not just Judeo-Christian Western culture that has scorned homosexual behavior; and 2) that in those (rare) cultures where homosexual behavior has *not* been scorned, gayness didn't stop at some hypothetical 10 percent, but ended up being virtually epidemic.

Homosexual behavior throughout a society is not static, but fluid. It can change radically in either direction, depending upon societal attitudes toward it. Isn't that what sexual taboos have always been about? Both society and the individual have a say in the matter.

Society can ban it or bless it; and whatever society decides, it is likely that its individual citizens will choose to go as far as they are permitted to go.

That's What the Bible Said All Along

If we take a close look at the account of Lot and the men of Sodom, we'll discover that the text says that "*all* the men from every part of the city of Sodom—both young and old—surrounded the house."[28] Not just 10 percent, but *all*. Even allowing for legitimate hyperbole, we're talking about a large segment of the population of Sodom. What ought to make us shudder about the future of our own nation is that, for the men of Sodom, sodomy was not *abnormal* but *normal*.

It bears repeating: A society can get so sexually liberated that what was once *abnormal* sexual behavior actually becomes *the norm*! And it is the gays themselves who remind us of that fact every time they bring up ancient Rome and Greece to show the "naturalness" of homosexual behavior. So why all the hypocritical pretense that social taboos are not effective in any event, or that the gay movement represents no threat to society's current morals?

Lessons from History

Lest we forget just how far a society can get mired down in sexual perversion, we need to hear again the words of William Barclay in his commentary on 1 Corinthians 6:9-11:

> We have left the most unnatural sin to the end—there were *homosexuals*. This sin had swept like a cancer through Greek life and from Greece, invaded Rome. We can scarcely realize how riddled the ancient world was with it. Even so great a man as Socrates practised it. Plato's dialogue *The Symposium* is always said to be one of the greatest works

on love in the world, but its subject is not natural but unnatural love.

Fourteen out of the first fifteen Roman emperors practised unnatural vice. At this very time Nero was emperor. He had taken a boy called Sporus and had him castrated. He then married him with a full marriage ceremony and took him home in procession to his palace and lived with him as wife. With an incredible viciousness, Nero had himself married a man called Pythagoras and called him his husband.

When Nero was eliminated and Otho came to the throne, one of the first things he did was to take possession of Sporus. Much later, the Emperor Hadrian's name was associated with a Bithynian youth called Antinous. He lived with him inseparably, and, when he died, he deified him and covered the world with his statues and immortalised his sin by calling a star after him.

In this particular vice, in the time of the Early Church, the world was lost to shame; and there can be little doubt that this was one of the main causes of its degeneracy and the final collapse of its civilization.[29]

What more proof do we need in order to realize that homosexual activity is not a static phenomenon inherent to some small percentage of the population which for a variety of complex reasons happens to be homosexually oriented? Unrestrained and aggressively promoted, homosexual behavior can easily become the sex of choice for an entire society.

Nor is homosexual behavior simply a matter of private sexual expression. It has social implications of the highest order. As ancient Greece and Rome warn us, nothing less than the survival of our civilization is at stake.

Out of the Mouths of Gays

One sometimes finds allies in the most surprising places. Imagine my shock upon first reading the words of gay activist Darrell Yates Rist in his article "Are Homosexuals Born That Way?" in *The Nation*: "I have found that even many of my most unbiased straight friends grow skiddish with my homosexual candor—say, kissing my mate—when their children are around. Underneath it all, they too understand that sexually free ideas are infectious and that, once introduced to the suggestion of same-sex love, their kids might just try it and like it."[30]

Even as a former district attorney, I don't recall ever hearing a more damning (or insightful) confession. Rist couldn't have said it better: Sexually free ideas *are* infectious! And everyone today knows what we must do when a rampant infection puts us at risk. If we're going to practice "safe society," then using legal prophylactics against gay rights is the only responsible course to take.

CHAPTER 8

The Dark Side
of Being Gay

A fag is a homosexual gentleman who has left the room.
—Truman Capote

This chapter is not for the squeamish. We leave behind the relatively neutral territory of homosexual orientation and enter the ugly landscape of what homosexual behavior is really all about. It's about the unthinkable and the inconceivable. We're no longer talking about a couple of guys reading poetry in the moonlight and holding hands. We're talking about "Queer Nation," drag queens, and Gay Pride Parades with shirtless grown men groping each other in front of women and children. It's about bathhouses and bedrooms where the unspeakable (and unprintable) take place.

And it's about pornography, homosexual style. Or "homoerotica," as it is called. It's not a pretty sight.

Strangely enough, gay activists are split on tactics. Some want to flaunt their homosexual behavior until we get so numbed by it that it becomes as acceptable as promiscuous heterosexual display and behavior. ("If it worked for Playboy and virtually every film, book, and advertiser who realizes that sex sells, then surely it will work for us!")

Others want a "kinder, gentler" approach, one that makes the soft sell. They want to make homosexuals look good. Normal. Like your next-door neighbors. Left to these slick marketing men, you would never guess what homosexuals actually do once they leave their Wall Street offices, step out of their BMW's, and depart the local restaurant after the traditional Sunday afternoon tea.

The gay strategy is clearly calculated: "In order to make a Gay Victim sympathetic to straights, you have to portray him as Everyman. To confound bigoted stereotypes and hasten the conversion of straights, strongly favorable images of gays must be set before the public."[1]

How is this going to happen? By shifting the focus away from how homosexuals *actually behave*—away from what homosexuals *actually do*:

> The main thing is to talk about gayness until the issue becomes thoroughly tiresome.
>
> And when we say *talk* about homosexuality, we mean just that. In the early stages of the campaign, the public should not be shocked and repelled by premature exposure to homo-*sexual* behavior itself. Instead, the imagery of sex per se should be downplayed, and the issue of gay rights reduced, as far as possible, to an abstract social question.[2]

The strategy? It's the same as with the abortion issue. Pro-abortionists *have* to talk abstractly about the right to choose. If anyone ever saw an actual abortion in progress it would bring an end to the entire debate right then and there! So too with gays, the argument *has* to be couched in terms of form over substance: "Turn up the rhetoric, but for heaven's sake don't let the people out there know what it actually is that we demand the right to do!"

So What DO They Do?

What do gays do? The answer depends to some extent upon which gays we are talking about. For starters, lesbians and homosexual men obviously do different things, much like the difference between what heterosexual men and heterosexual women tend to do. Lesbians, on the whole, are more partnered and relationship-oriented; gay men are more promiscuous and physically oriented. So lesbian sex is not necessarily genitally focused. But some lesbians do revert to wanting heterosexual-like intercourse, and therefore use dildos (rubber and plastic imitations) to simulate normal sex. That way they can play it both ways.

Then we must separate out those gays who are in long-standing relationships. The older set, particularly, are a different breed from the younger gay men on the streets. Just up the lane in my village in England, for example, there are two men of retirement age whom everyone refers to as "the boys." By every indication they are gay. Both men are stable and well-respected in their professions and also by the villagers. One never gets the idea that they are out each night cruising gay bars.

Nevertheless, it has to be said that homosexual conduct is morally reprehensible in whatever form it takes. There are no "morally respectable" ways to have gay sex. But when you put the spotlight on the large class of *promiscuous* male homosexuals, what *they* do is quite unbelievable!

A Different Kind of Promiscuity

One should not be fooled by the word *promiscuous*, as if there were no difference between heterosexual and homosexual promiscuity. Neither is biblically justified, but homosexual promiscuity is a different phenomenon altogether. With heterosexual promiscuity, under most circumstances there is at least the *pretense* of "wooing" (dinner dates, flowers, candy, etc.). Even in straight singles bars (where you can forget the flowers and candy), there is some attempt at small talk and romancing, if

perhaps greatly abbreviated. Even in its worst manifestations, heterosexual promiscuity still involves a
process of persuasion in which there is an escalation of
shared intimacy before sexual pleasure is reached. Given
all that, the world of heterosexual promiscuity simply
has no equivalent of the gay sauna![3]

Flowers and candy would be a mockery to what goes
on in gay bars, bookstores, and saunas. The back room
often provides cubicles where total strangers meet for
oral sex and mutual masturbation. There is no pretense
of relationship, and not the slightest masquerade of emotional involvement. And persuasion is hardly the word
for gay "cruising."

Gay psychotherapist Joe Brewer says that homosexual
sex is made all the more promiscuous because there is
"nobody to say 'no'—no moderating role like that a
woman plays in the heterosexual milieu."[4] Even in a
promiscuous heterosexual world, the woman is still
likely to put on the brakes. Among homosexual males,
by contrast, the absence of a woman's moderating influence leaves only a crotch mentality.

So when we speak of homosexual promiscuity, it's a
whole new ball game. We're talking gay bars where men
dance lasciviously and fondle each other. We're talking
multiple-partnered sex over the course of an evening,
with other men whose names are not even known—
sometimes up to a dozen partners a night. It's anal. It's
oral. It's any kinky way you can do it. It's body kissing
and nipple nibbling. It's dildos, douches, vibrators, butt
plugs, bondage, beating, whipping, and spanking. It's
dripping hot candle wax onto the skin. It's the "circle
jerk." It's the "glory holes" in bathroom stalls just made
for anonymous oral sex.

When it comes to what gays *do*, the military is getting
ready to pull out all stops, if necessary, to tell what really
goes on in the barracks when gays play army. According
to *Newsweek*:

Military officials are gathering case histories of gay behavior in the armed services in an attempt to prove rampant promiscuity. Pro-ban advocates within the military are prodding army investigators to release a film they have of army soldiers and civilians in Ft. Hood, Texas, mutually masturbating in a latrine. Efforts to get copies of it to make public have been unsuccessful, and a senior army official says, "It's being protected like the gold in Fort Knox."[5]

Among the more kinky set, we're talking about "water sports" and "golden showers" (acts of urination); shared douches and enemas; rimming or tonguing (of the anus); ingestion of fecal matter; and "fisting" (where the hand, fist, or forearm is inserted into the rectum). And unless I had read it from a reliable source, I would never have believed that there could be such a thing as the practice of "gerbilizing" or "gerbil shooting," where a live rodent is inserted into the anus.[6]

No wonder doctors are regularly called in to treat the medical side effects of such bizarre behavior. In fact, they see colon problems so often among homosexual males that they even have what they call the "gay bowel syndrome" to describe a group of parasitic, viral, and bacterial infections prevalent among homosexual men. That doesn't count the damage done to the rectum itself from all the abnormal antics that gays perform. (When the gerbil can't find its way out and dies in the struggle, surgery is sometimes made necessary.)

So let's not hear any more of the cry, "It's none of your business what we do sexually." As taxpayers, it very well *is* our business! Just ask your local fireman or paramedic what it is costing taxpayers to have all the emergency runs that are made each day to mop up after gays have played their kinky games. This sordidness may be *done in private*, but it's *the public* that pays.

When one sees what gays perform with each other, the argument about some inherent, biological homosexual orientation proves itself to be a pile of garbage. Forget the images beamed into our living rooms of the loving gay couple who look after each other in their twilight years. Homosexual sex is nothing less than moral corruption and degradation. The practice of sodomy has its own progeny: Perversion begets perversion.

Naturally, gay activists hate it when we bring all this up.

Playthings for Pedophiles

What gay activists hate even more than any of the foregoing is any mention of *pedophilia* in the same sentence with *homosexual behavior*. The last thing gays want us to think about is any connection between homosexuals and children. Any such connection obviously puts homosexuals in an unfavorable light, whether we are considering gays who might wish to adopt, or who work in the field of child care, or even when moral legitimacy is at stake.

It is argued by gays that there is no more sexual abuse of young children than by heterosexuals. And heaven knows there is plenty of abuse by heterosexuals. But gays are in trouble right off the bat on this issue, partly because of efforts by gay activists to either lower the age of consent for homosexual relations or to abolish age limits altogether. Why should either of those be an objective of the gay movement if there is no truth to the rumor that many homosexuals seek out adolescents for fulfillment of their sexual fantasies?

And are we simply to ignore what gays themselves say about the relationship between younger and older homosexuals? Consider, for example, this frank admission:

Nobody is fooled when we proclaim that the gay movement has nothing to do with kids and

their sexuality. . . . Many of us—both women
and men—had our first homosexual experience with partners who were older than ourselves.[7]

What ages are we talking about? When the Paedophile
Information Exchange in Britain carried out a survey of
their membership, they found that men were most often
interested in boys from ten to thirteen.[8]

And how are young people recruited? There is always
the "Gay Helpline" which advertises for the young to
call if they are having conflicts or questions about their
homosexuality. Callers are directed to gay organizations
and clubs where they are easy prey for older homosexuals always looking for nubile young bodies. Gay counseling is nothing if not a channel for young people struggling with their sexual orientation. You can bet they are
not set up to dissuade the hesitant.

Male Prostitutes—A Necessity for Old Gays

The proverbial mid-life crisis can be far more stressful
for gays than for heterosexuals. For homosexuals, youth
is everything. Former gay Frank Worthen recalls his
days in the San Francisco gay scene: "There were bars
where they checked your ID and if you were 40 you
couldn't get in. It got to be pretty lonely."[9]

When you understand how sex among homosexuals
is focused upon youth and good looks, you begin to
understand how young boys often get caught up in the
web of homosexuals for hire. In fact, homosexual prostitutes of any age become a virtual necessity for older
gays, who themselves have lost their youth or good
looks. Unless older gays are partnered, rent-boys become their best option for sexual outlet.

Consider this acknowledgment in the Gay Liberation
Front Manifesto:

> Gay men are very apt to fall victim to the cult of youth—those sexual parades in the "glamorous" meat-rack bars of London and New York, those gay beaches of the South of France and Los Angeles haven't anything to do with liberation. Those are the hang-outs of the plastic gays who are obsessed with image and appearance. In love with their own bodies, these gay men dread the approach of age, because to be old is to be "ugly," and with their youth they lose also the right to love and be loved, and are valued only if they can pay.[10]

Little wonder that the legalization of homosexual prostitution is invariably part of the gay agenda. Even more than heterosexuals bent on pleasure for pay, homosexuals have a vested interested in sex for sale.

Homoerotica—Crucial to the Gay Food Chain

The gay porn industry is what keeps much of the activity going. Adult bookstores are full of it. (In fact, the bookstores serve almost like "churches" for gays in search of fun and fellowship.) Why is homoerotica so important? Because homoerotica is food for thought. Food for lustful *homosexual* thought, to be precise. Not that there isn't plenty of heterosexual pornography available on the racks in adult bookstores and minimarkets. But homoerotica seems to always go "one better." It specializes in shock value and majors in being offensive.

Perhaps more importantly (just as with heterosexuals), homoerotica substitutes as foreplay where there is no normal romantic relationship to make it happen naturally. When sex is only physical and not relational, it can take a bit of revving up.

Gay porn also satisfies the typically *selfish* sexual instincts of the homosexual mind. With gay porn, a man doesn't have to share love with a woman, nor even with another man. Through the visual arts, a man can love just himself if he wants to. Sometimes there's less hassle that way—and today, of course, less risk.

Lesbians and Homoerotica

It should really come as no surprise that, by comparison with male homoerotica, there is relatively little commercialized female homoerotica—at least directed at or consumed by lesbians. Lesbian and feminist artists do treat their respective subjects through their work, but even this (much to their chagrin) rarely surfaces.

Even when women are portrayed as "loving other women" in the legitimate art world, it is almost exclusively presented with relative taste and sensitivity—not grossly, as in male homoerotica. What is portrayed is an extension of the female bonding that is characteristic of women wholly apart from romantic or sexual expression. For women, the line between the two has always been much more blurred than with men.

The previously indicated differences between lesbians and gay men undoubtedly explains why, among lesbians, there is less focus (almost none by comparison with gay men) on the visual images that men often rely on to feed their sexual appetites.

Ironically, there is plenty of lesbian porn available in magazines, books, and films, but typically it is directed at and consumed by heterosexual men—usually heterosexual men who would be repulsed by *male* homosexual behavior!

The Fine Art of Homoerotica

Of course, male homoerotica is not confined to sleazy bookshelves in sleazy bookstores. In fact, the more shocking examples are now being shown at your local art gallery—hailed by the art world with such accolades as "powerful," "filled with symbolism," and "making a profound statement about the human condition." A prime example of this "powerful" artistic expression is Robert Mapplethorpe's controversial photograph of a white man with his fist inserted into the rectum of a black man. Among homosexuals who practice it, the act is known as "fisting." Mapplethorpe (a homosexual who has since died from AIDS) explained his reason for exposing such outrage to public view, saying that it represented a form of political expression. Sure.

In October 1990, a four-man and four-woman jury in the traditionally conservative city of Cincinnati was asked to decide whether the Contemporary Arts Center, along with its director, Dennis Barrie, was guilty of criminal obscenity charges stemming from the display of seven photographs by Mapplethorpe which were part of the 175-piece exhibit called "The Perfect Moment." The photographs in question depicted: a finger inserted into a penis; a man urinating into the mouth of another man; two photos of children, a boy and a girl, with their genitals showing; and three photos showing anal penetration with a bull whip, a cylinder, and, as mentioned above, a man's fist and arm.

The defense argued that the photos, while disturbing, were endowed with artistic value. To prove the point, the defense attorneys called numerous expert witnesses to attest to the artistic value of the pieces in controversy. Janet Kardon, who initially put the exhibit together, gave the following response on cross-examination by the prosecution:

> Prosecution: "What are the formal values of the picture where the finger is inserted in the penis?"
> Kardon: "It's a central image, very symmetrical, a very ordered, classic composition."[11]

When asked about the photo depicting "fisting," Kardon disingenuously compared its composition to one of Mapplethorpe's images of flowers.[12]

Robert Sobieszek managed a new low in pretzel logic by saying, "If it's in an art museum, it is intended to be art, and that is why it's there." By that definition, the proprietor of Joe's Adult Books and Peep Shows could avoid being hassled by the police simply by changing his sign to read: Joe's Art Museum!

Still another witness, Jacquelyn Baas, director of the University Art Museum in Berkeley, California, commented: "It's the tension between the physical beauty of the photographs and the brutal nature of what's going on in it."[13]

One wonders whether there is to be more outrage at the "brutal nature of what's going on" among gays, or at those in the nongay community who aid and abet their obscene behavior and the public depiction of it. Of course, many (though by no means all or even most) of those in the art world who are coming forward as advocates of homoerotic art are themselves gay and therefore have more than a passing interest in its existence.

Certainly, none of this is new—only for our "Christian nation." Looking back in history, we see great frescoes, paintings, urns, and assorted other bits of pottery decorated with scenes of nudity, copulation, sodomy, and even bestiality. (Despite all the protestations about such comparisons, what does that tell us about where the progression of libertine sex can eventually lead?)

But the fact that homoerotic art is not new is no excuse. All it says is that our society is becoming as morally barbaric as pagan societies which proceeded us and have now gone the way of all flesh—perhaps for that very reason!

Oh, the verdict in the Cincinnati case? "Not Guilty!" All around the country, lovers of porn art wept with joy.

Free Speech, Not Subsidized Porn

The worst part about all this high-class porn is that your tax dollars have been the expensive hooks upon which such "art" has been hung in the name of free expression. It all happened through the federally funded National Endowment for the Arts (NEA). Over its 20-year life (from 1970) its budget swelled from 8 million dollars to 173 million. By the late '70's it was funding a "representative range of American art" through grants to minority artists, including gays and lesbians.

It was then that Donald W. Wildmon (founder of the American Family Association) and Senator Jesse Helms of North Carolina launched an all-out assault on the NEA. In one of the few really tangible successes that can be listed in the column of Christian activism, NEA was brought to its senses.

At the cornerstone of NEA reforms was an oath required of all those applying for NEA grants, indicating their understanding that the NEA is prohibited from funding "obscene materials including but not limited to depictions of sadomasochism, homoeroticism, the exploitation of children, or individuals engaged in sex acts."

Naturally, the oath was vilified as a McCarthy-like "loyalty oath," and cries of censorship are still echoing in the marble hallways of the Capitol. Typical of the resulting outrage were such statements as, "Gay and lesbian artists face the imminent evisceration of our right to read, our right to write, our right to earn a living, and our right to free expression as Americans."[14]

That complaint slightly overstates the case. What the changes signaled was: You can paint, draw, sculpt, and write anything you want. But the rest of us don't have to pay for your porn. You have a Constitutional right to express yourself in every twisted way you wish, but don't ask us to finance your filth. Remember what you are asking for: it's *free* speech, not *subsidized* speech.

And then there's the matter of public display. Is the indecent exposure on the street by the sleazy guy in the dirty raincoat okay as long as he holds up a sign saying, "This is art"? Surely, if indecency is offensive on the street, it ought to be equally indecent in public museums.

Unfortunately, it's not likely that any of this will be the least bit persuasive to Bill Clinton, who is said to favor "depoliticizing" federal funding of the arts.[15] (Loosely translated, that means we can expect a return to tax-payer-subsidized homoerotica.)

The Dark Side of Guilt

Like Robert Mapplethorpe, controversial sculptor Robert Gober is also gay. His surreal art shocks the senses through that which is vile. Of his work, London art critic Richard Dorment says: "His work is truly decadent, but it is unforgettable."[16] I suppose that begs the question: Do we want to be exposed to decadence that we can never forget?

But there may indeed be some "social redeeming value" (to use the formula by which the courts have rescued various obscenities) to Gober's art. Perhaps through his work you and I can get some insight into the incomparable guilt which accompanies the dark side of gayness. And from what we've seen in this chapter alone, surely it must be a heavy burden indeed.

Dorment tells us that "to understand [Gober's] work, we need to know two or three fundamental things about his life. [He was] born in 1954 into a devoutly Roman Catholic family. . . . He is also gay, which means that he has been surrounded by the dead and dying for a large part of his adult life."

Having given us that personal background, Dorment describes some of Gober's art, which includes sensuously modeled plaster sculptures that look like white kitchen sinks, complete with plug holes:

> The exhibition is, finally, about the living hell of being Robert Gober. Its anger at the predicament life has placed him in is almost uncontrollable, and, what is more, it is drenched in moral guilt.
>
> Gober's sinks were about a fantasy, the fantasy that sexual guilt can be physically washed away, that sin can be made to vanish down the drain.[17]

I suppose the cynic could always say of Gober's great sense of guilt, "Well, what else would you expect? He was brought up Catholic!" But what of all the non-Catholic gays who exhibit the telltale signs of overwhelming guilt? What about the higher-than-average suicide rate? The notorious drug and alcohol abuse? The endless therapy sessions? It can't all be laid at the feet of the Pope. Or even homophobia.

What we are seeing through Gober—maybe even through Mapplethorpe—is the acting out of guilt on behalf of all homosexuals. Orientation or no orientation, they can't live with themselves for what they do. And that alone speaks volumes about the *choice* involved in their behavior.

By their guilt, homosexuals acknowledge the volitional nature of their behavior. By their shame, homosexuals confess to themselves that what they are doing is wrong.

It is not just us that they are trying desperately to convince of their moral innocence. It is themselves! In their guilt-stained consciences, they join with Lady Macbeth when she uttered the wrenching words of unwashed guilt: "Yet here's a spot. Out, damn'd spot!"

Like Lady Macbeth, and Pilate in his own day, Gober attempts to wash away his own sins. But his plaster sinks will never have enough drains to rid himself of the guilt for a lifestyle he knows to be sinful. How long will tormented homosexuals persist in imagining that "confessional" homoerotic art or—worse yet—"gay pride" can root out the psychological and spiritual demons that haunt them?

Or is it, in fact, that the church has issued a subtle decree that homosexual behavior is "the unforgivable sin"? Is *that* why gays are never able to free themselves from the dark side of evil? Because we've told them through both our teaching and our attitudes that it's impossible?

If we are truly Christians, sinners all, then surely we must know that the message of the cross is as much a message of hope to gays as it is to the vilest of the vile. What can wash away their sins? *Nothing!* Nothing, that is, but the blood of Jesus.

> *Wash away all my iniquity and cleanse me from my sin. For I know my transgressions, and my sin is always before me. . . . Cleanse me with hyssop, and I will be clean; wash me, and I will be whiter than snow.*[18]

CHAPTER 9

Scripturephobic Bible-Bashing

'Twas guilt that taught my heart to fear,
And pride my fears relieved;
How precious did that pride appear,
The hour I first believed!
—Revised lyrics to "Amazing Grace" as sung at San Francisco's (gay) Glide Memorial United Methodist Church.

In the gay-rights assault against the American culture, no citadel is more coveted than the church. Getting the church's imprimatur on the homosexual lifestyle would be the ultimate stamp of legitimacy. But no matter how seductive that idea is for many mainstream churches—in keeping with the spirit of Christian tolerance and love—there is always that one last hurdle to cross: the Bible.

Have you ever wondered how gays attempt to get around the many passages in the Bible that condemn homosexual conduct as sin? Those who pay homage to the Bible (most don't even bother) have become incredibly sophisticated in the unholy art of sidestepping God's revelation.

In his book *Just As I Am—A Practical Guide to Being Out, Proud, and Christian*, pro-gay theologian Robert Williams attempts a biblical justification of homosexual conduct by asking, "What's the most loving course of action? What would Christ have you do?" As implied in the perversely fashioned title to his book, the most loving thing to do is what Christ himself would do: Accept gays *just as they are*.

He then tells us what we already knew, that "without interpretation, without placing it in its cultural, historical, and literary context, the Bible can be used for evil."[1] And from that point forward, Williams proceeds to demonstrate the very evil of which he speaks by systematically reconstructing each and every passage which threatens his freedom to enjoy homosexual relations.

As for the whole of the Pauline letters, Williams highhandedly concludes: "What the Holy Spirit tells you is a greater authority for *your* life than what the Holy Spirit may or may not have told Paul."[2]

In the Footsteps of Feminists

To get around obvious biblical proscriptions against homosexual acts, pro-gay theology borrows heavily from feminist theology. It's basically a matter of *hermeneutics*. If that's a new word for you, it simply refers to the *method* whereby we read, interpret, and apply Scripture. Not everyone wears the same set of glasses when they open their Bibles. Recently, in order to get around the numerous passages that expressly call for different roles for men and women in the church, feminist theologians have taken to radical, revisionist methods of interpreting Scripture.

For example, Elisabeth Schussler Fiorenza, a New Testament scholar and author of *Bread Not Stone: The Challenge of Feminist Biblical Interpretation*, promotes what she calls a *hermeneutic of suspicion*, a hermeneutic which rejects any biblical text that appears to have a patriarchal bias.[3] With that, she blithely dismisses the gender distinctions called for in Paul's writings.

To a lesser extent (undoubtedly because there are fewer Scriptures with which to take issue), black activists have done the same thing. James Cone, the black theologian of liberation, asserts that "any interpretation of the gospel in any historical period that fails to see Jesus as the Liberator of the oppressed is heretical."[4] And with that, Paul's instructions that slaves be content with their lot in life are scissored out of Scripture.

Whether gay, feminist, or black activist, today's cultural priests and priestesses are applying radical, revisionist, and reconstructionist approaches to the biblical text, with predictable, self-serving results. Their method? Imaginative narrative interpretation, or "reading between the lines."

Feminist author Dorothee Solle (*Beyond Mere Obedience*) calls the method *phantasie* (German for phantasy), a process of creative imagining—not passive escapism, but an active imaging of the possibilities within a given text.[5] Robert Williams explains:

> The technique is simply one of creative visualization. You select a biblical passage, read it carefully and thoughtfully, then close the Bible and allow yourself to *experience* the passage. It works best with narrative passages, such as those in the gospels. . . . .
>
> As with any visualization, the secret is to set the scene as vividly as possible. When you close your eyes and imagine the setting you just read about, imagine it in the most intense detail you can muster. Pay attention to colors, sounds, smells. Notice what people are wearing, what color their eyes and hair are, what their facial expressions are.[6]

Using such creative visualization, Williams informs us that David and Jonathan were gay lovers;[7] that the story of Ruth and Naomi is "the account of a deeply committed, intergenerational, lesbian love affair;"[8] and that—yes—Jesus himself was a homosexual! After all, "the disciple whom Jesus loved" *was* close by in the upper room, "snuggled up against Jesus' chest." . . .[9]

In previous generations this form of hermeneutical interpretation was called by another name—*blasphemy!*

The Old Testament Through Revisionist Glasses

Gays realize that they must deal with the whole of Scripture if they are to have any chance of convincing us—or themselves—that homosexual conduct is pleasing in the eyes of God. It's a daunting task, but they set forth in confidence, undeterred by even the most explicit biblical teaching. It begins at Creation, where they know that the most fundamental principles of gender, marriage, and sex are established.

Genesis 1:28

> God blessed them and said to them, "Be fruitful and increase in number; fill the earth and subdue it. Rule over the fish of the sea and the birds of the air and over every living creature that moves on the ground."

With this opening passage, gay theology goes for the jugular of Roman Catholic teaching on sex: that sex is for the purpose of procreation. Gays answer weakly that they sometimes *do* procreate, either before "turning gay," or as bisexuals, or through alternative technologies (e.g., lesbians being artificially inseminated).

On firmer territory, they bask in a false sense of correctness, due to the weakness of the Catholic interpretation of this passage. Neither here nor elsewhere does the Bible teach that procreation is the *only* purpose of sexual relations.

Where gays go wrong on this point is in assuming that the pleasure which God intended sex to bring in addition to the act of procreation is without moral limitations. Procreation, requiring as it does both male and female, is as defining of proper sexual relations as it is of procreative roles. It's not just male and female for reproduction; it's also male and female for legitimate sexual enjoyment.

Genesis 2:24

> For this reason a man will leave his father and mother and be united to his wife, and they will become one flesh.

All it takes for gays to make this passage gender neutral is the simple replacement of the word *companion* for the word *wife*. That the woman was made to be "a helper" for man suggests the idea of companionship, say gay theologians, and not just a difference in gender. By pro-gay thinking, loving companionship of any type is what God wants, for truly "it is not good for man to be alone."

It should be enough to point out that this convenient translation is nothing more than taking the liberty of literally rewriting Scripture. God neither created another *man* for Adam's companion, nor a third person of either sex, as if to indicate the insignificance of gender. It was to be one *man* (male) and one *woman* (female) for life. Man would have his "companions," as would woman, but not for sexual expression.

Genesis 19:1-13,24,25

> The two angels arrived at Sodom in the evening, and Lot was sitting in the gateway of the city. When he saw them, he got up to meet them and bowed down with his face to the ground. "My lords," he said, "please turn aside to your servant's house. You can wash your feet and spend the night and then go on your way early in the morning."

"No," they answered, "we will spend the night in the square."

But he insisted so strongly that they did go with him and entered his house. He prepared a meal for them, baking bread without yeast, and they ate.

Before they had gone to bed, all the men from every part of the city of Sodom—both young and old—surrounded the house. They called to Lot, "Where are the men who came to you tonight? Bring them out to us so that we can have sex with them."

Lot went outside to meet them and shut the door behind him and said, "No, my friends. Don't do this wicked thing. Look, I have two daughters who have never slept with a man. Let me bring them out to you, and you can do what you like with them. But don't do anything to these men, for they have come under the protection of my roof."

"Get out of our way," they replied. And they said, "This fellow came here as an alien, and now he wants to play the judge! We'll treat you worse than them." They kept bringing pressure on Lot and moved forward to break down the door.

But the men inside reached out and pulled Lot back into the house and shut the door. Then they struck the men who were at the door of the house, young and old, with blindness so that they could not find the door. The two men said to Lot, "Do you have anyone else here—sons-in-law, sons or daughters, or anyone else in the city who belongs to you? Get them out of here, because we are going to destroy this place. The outcry to the LORD against its people is so great that he has sent us to destroy it. . . ."

Then the LORD rained down burning sulfur on Sodom and Gomorrah—from the LORD out of the heavens. Thus he overthrew those cities and the entire plain, including all those living in the cities—and also the vegetation in the land.

This passage is so definitive of homosexual conduct that our modern-day reference to *sodomy* is based on it. No wonder gay theologians are anxious to minimize its impact any way they can! Whatever the men of Sodom were up to, there is no question but that it drew God's wrath!

The first line of attack for all revisionists is to cast doubt on the meaning of the translated word when compared with the original. Pro-gay theologians therefore point out that the Hebrew verb *yadah*, translated in the King James Version "to know," may either mean "get to know" or be a euphemism for sex (as in "carnal knowledge" or "he *knew* her in a biblical sense").

The latter usage, "to have sex with," is adopted in the New International Version, quoted above. However, we are told that such a meaning is unlikely, since the word is used in the Hebrew Scriptures 943 times, and in only ten of those does it have the connotation of "carnal knowledge."

I suppose one would be foolish to ask how, using the same logic, one can be sure that *yadah* meant "having sex" in the ten cases cited. Couldn't the same argument be used in each case?

And what are we to make of any consistent interpretation of *yadah* in verse 8, which the King James version renders, "I have two daughters which have not *known* man"? Are we to presume that Lot's daughters were "not acquainted with" any men? Surely the point was that they were *virgins*, never having *had sex* with a man. As used in each case, *yadah* contemplated sexual relations.

More to the point, the context simply defies any other interpretation. Are we supposed to believe that the men of Sodom were rebuked by Lot for merely wanting to make the acquaintance of the visitors? Are we being asked to believe that God rained down fire from heaven because the men of Sodom comprised some kind of a Chamber of Commerce welcoming committee?

Pro-gay theology responds that it was *violence* for which the men of Sodom were condemned, not homosexual sex. Williams goes so far as to say that "virtually all mainstream biblical scholars, including those who are somewhat conservative, agree that the point of the story, the 'sin of Sodom,' is not about sex, but about violence."

I've had enough courtroom experience to know that one can always find an "expert" to testify in his behalf on virtually any position imaginable, but I must demand a "bill of particulars" on this one. What "conservative," even "mainstream" scholars are we talking about? I've consulted a number of respectable conservative and mainstream scholars on Genesis 19, and so far I have found none who would take issue with the assertion that the "sin of Sodom" encompassed the sin of homosexual conduct, whether or not violently intended.

Certainly, Sodom's wickedness was not exclusively related to homosexual conduct. Even before the two angels visited Lot, Abraham was negotiating with God over the wickedness that was endemic in Sodom. And, writing centuries later, Ezekiel the prophet notes that Sodom's wickedness included pride, materialism, and injustice:

> Now this was the sin of your sister Sodom: She and her daughters were arrogant, overfed and unconcerned; they did not help the poor and needy.[10]

But never doubt that Ezekiel's dirty laundry list on Sodom included other "detestable" sins as well:

> They were haughty and did detestable things before me. Therefore I did away with them as you have seen.[11]

In an attempt to shift the blame away from its homosexual implications, Genesis 19 is presented by pro-gay theologians as preaching the sin of *inhospitality*, and that therefore "when a family or a church group disowns one of its members after discovering his or her homosexuality, *they* are committing the sin of sodomy. When Cardinal O'Connor preaches against gay rights, he is committing the sin of sodomy."[12]

Certainly there is no justification for shunning the penitent sinner, but Lot was saved from Sodom's destruction precisely because he called sin *sin*, no matter how "inhospitable" or "intolerant" it seemed to those who were bent on flaunting sin in the sight of God.

On its face, a more difficult problem posed by pro-gay theologians concerns Lot's offer to give over to the men of Sodom his two virgin daughters. That offer (as well as a similar one made in the strikingly parallel story of the Levite in Judges 19) does indeed shock one's modern sensibilities. Williams says, "Lot's lack of concern for his daughters ought to render this story useless as a moral and ethical model!"

As uncomfortable as we might feel about Lot's offer of his daughters, the one thing we cannot say is that the story is "useless as a moral and ethical model." In his short New Testament letter, the inspired writer Jude employs the incident as exactly that—a moral model—specifically naming "sexual immorality and perversion" as the sin for which God brought down his judgment.[13] Peter does likewise in his second epistle.[14]

We may never feel good about the moral propriety of offering the daughters. Yet one cannot help but wonder if the enigmatic reference to Lot's daughters is simply to further highlight the kind of sex the men of Sodom were after. Unlike the wicked Benjamites in Judges 19, who saw the Levite's concubine as a "consolation prize" and raped her to the point of death, the men of Sodom weren't after just any kind of sex. Rape alone was not good enough for the Sodomites. It was *perverse sex only* that they demanded.

Deuteronomy 23:17,18

> No Israelite man or woman is to become a shrine prostitute. You must not bring the earnings of a female prostitute or of a male prostitute into the house of the LORD your God to pay any vow, because the LORD your God detests them both.

Initially, pro-gay advocates objected to the King James translation, which used the words "sodomite" and "dog" in reference to the male cult prostitutes. But even the modern translations, as above, leave gay critics unsatisfied: "The sex, whether homosexual, heterosexual, or transvestitism, was not the issue; the issue was idolatry."[15]

As for the passage's focus on idolatry, the point is well taken. But any inverse implication—that male prostitution itself is somehow thereby legitimized—is a kind of tortured logic in which only someone desperate for self-justification can indulge.

Leviticus 18:22

> Do not lie with a man as one lies with a woman; that is detestable.

What pro-gay theologians say of this explicit passage ought to win some kind of award for creativity! "The operative and telling phrase here," says Robert Williams, "is *as with a woman*." He goes on to explain that the prohibition is not against having same-gender sex, but against having it in any manner that would perpetuate class distinction. In other words, a man should not have sex with another man in the degrading way in which men have sex with women, treating them as inferiors. As long as sex is enjoyed with mutual respect, it doesn't matter who is doing what with whom!

Are we to take it that the same explanation applies to the very next verse?

> Do not have sexual relations with an animal and defile yourself with it. A woman must not present herself to an animal to have sexual relations with it; that is a perversion.

I appreciate how unfair it is to bring up bestiality in the same sentence as homosexuality, but the absurdity of the "class distinction" explanation for verse 22 is exploded by even the most cursory look at verse 23.

The Levitical prohibition neither assumes that heterosexual sex deems the woman to be man's social inferior nor that any amount of mutuality between two members of the same gender would legitimize sex between them.

In this regard it is interesting to note the penalty attached to the prohibition. Leviticus 20:13 instructs that "if a man lies with a man as one lies with a woman, *both of them* have done what is detestable. *They* must be put to death; *their* blood will be on their own heads." The punishment had nothing to do with "class distinctions." It assumed that *both* men were doing *with each other* that which was detestable.

As a last-ditch effort to get around the plain teaching of this passage, gays make a feeble attempt at damage control. They point to other prohibitions which were considered "abominations" (to use the King James terminology for "detestable"), including various "unclean" dietary foods,[16] different forms of idolatry,[17] blemished sacrifices,[18] acts of divination,[19] remarrying a divorced wife,[20] and even "haughty eyes" and "a lying tongue," in the words of Proverbs.[21]

Of course, it's a "this sin is no worse than any other sin" argument—which is true as far as it goes. All sin is an affront to God. The problem for gays (and for any of the rest of us, for that matter) is that such an argument never goes far enough to make any sin "not a sin," as they try to imply, and that is the ultimate, futile aim of pro-gay theologians.

Culturally Updating the New Testament

What you run into in discussing New Testament passages with pro-gay theologians is a hermeneutical ploy that introduces "the cultural argument." At the center of the argument stands the apostle Paul, who—so it is said—is writing either from his own personal biases or who reflects the patriarchal standards of his day.

This cultural argument goes on to say that times have changed, and with them God's will. *"Their* story" in the first century is not *"our* story" today. Paul's perspective is no longer relevant; it is out of step with the twentieth century. Scripture must constantly be updated so that it can minister to the needs of people in whatever circumstances they may be found. And with that hermeneutical approach, we once again see both radical reinterpretation of familiar texts and something new—the sheer rejection of biblical authority!

Again, Robert Williams says it most chillingly: "The point is not really whether or not some passage in the Bible condemns homosexual acts; the point is that you cannot allow your moral and ethical decisions to be determined by the literature of a people whose culture and history are so far removed from your own. You must dare to be iconoclastic enough to say, 'So what if the Bible does say it? Who cares?'"[22]

Romans 1:18,19; 24-27

The wrath of God is being revealed from heaven against all the godlessness and wickedness of men who suppress the truth by their wickedness, since what may be known about God is plain to them, because God has made it plain to them. . . .

Therefore God gave them over in the sinful desires of their hearts to sexual impurity for the degrading of their bodies with one another. They exchanged the truth of God for a lie, and worshiped and served created things rather than the Creator—who is forever praised. Amen.

Because of this, God gave them over to shameful lusts. Even their women exchanged natural relations for unnatural ones. In the same way the men also abandoned natural relations with women and were inflamed with lust for one another. Men committed indecent acts with other men, and received in themselves the due penalty for their perversion.

This is a particularly painful passage for gays. And especially so for lesbians, since it is the only passage making direct reference to female homosexuals.

Initial protest is made that the passage seems to blame homosexuality on the idolatrous practice of worshiping "created things rather than the Creator." But here Paul seems not to be thinking specifically of wooden idols or stone gods of some kind—only the fact that homosexual conduct, like all other sin, *dethrones God* (the Creator) and *enthrones man* (the creature).

The primary assault comes against the obvious implications for homosexuals: that homosexual conduct is "unnatural." That's the *last* thing gays would ever want to hear the Bible say about what they do. To be absolved of responsibility for their sexual acts, they absolutely must prove that what they do is completely natural in every sense of the term.

It's a question of whether Paul was right in saying that homosexual acts stem from "sinful desires of the heart" and "shameful lusts." If Paul was right, then homosexual acts are plainly sinful and subject to God's condemnation. So the stakes are high, and everything possible must be done to favorably explain what Paul means by "unnatural."

Their best shot is similar to their attack on Leviticus 18:22. Says Williams, "It is precisely the social equality of the sexual partners that causes Paul to label same-sex relations 'unnatural.' Sex that was 'natural,' in Paul's view, necessarily involved males dominating females!"[23]

This hardly needs refuting. Even Williams realizes that any attempt to get around the plain meaning of Paul's words is hopeless. So he turns to decanonizing the passage altogether: "Perhaps Paul is condemning homosexuality in this passage, or at least labeling it as 'unnatural' (which is not *exactly* the same thing as calling it sinful). But the bottom line for you is: So what? Paul was wrong about a number of other things, too. Why should you take him any more seriously than you take Jerry Falwell or Anita Bryant or Cardinal O'Connor?"[24]

Well, there we have the real truth of the matter: Who cares what the Bible says if it disagrees with what we believe or want to do! And from there it just goes downhill altogether.

1 Corinthians 6:9,10

> Do you not know that the wicked will not inherit the kingdom of God? Do not be deceived: Neither the sexually immoral nor idolaters nor adulterers nor male prostitutes nor homosexual offenders nor thieves nor the greedy nor drunkards nor slanderers nor swindlers will inherit the kingdom of God.

1 Timothy 1:9-11

> We also know that law is made not for the righteous but for lawbreakers and rebels, the ungodly and sinful, the unholy and irreligious; for those who kill their fathers or mothers, for murderers, for adulterers and perverts, for slave traders and liars and perjurers—and for whatever else is contrary to the sound doctrine that conforms to the glorious gospel of the blessed God, which he entrusted to me.

After quibbling about the various words translated in these two lists of sinners—whether "sodomites," "sexual perverts," "sexually immoral," "male prostitutes," or "homosexual offenders"—gay theologians finally throw up their hands in despair.

For Williams, there is nothing left but to say, "Paul, like most of us, had his good moments and his bad moments."[25] And then he takes us back to the feminist test of canonicity: *"It cannot be believed unless it rings true to our deepest capacity for truth and goodness."*[26] With that, he concludes: "Any discussion of the household of God, then, that degenerates into a list of those who will not get into the club should strike you as misguided. It does not ring true to our deepest capacity for truth and goodness. This passage, then, simply has no authority for you."[27]

Here we go again. Take what feels good from the Bible and dump the rest of it! So why all the pretense at scholarly debate over the meaning of individual biblical passages? Why even bother opening the Bible in the first place?

Once we ourselves become the highest moral authority, the Bible is irrelevant at best and a nuisance at worst. Williams, writing to fellow homosexuals, makes no bones about it: "As a queer Christian, you can draw from other sources, particularly from the sacred writings of your own people, past and present, as well as from the 'rather grossly overrated' Bible."

Up Close and Personal

Throughout this chapter I have purposely chosen to liberally quote from Robert Williams even though there are many other sources available at my fingertips. By now the basic arguments are fairly standardized. However, for a reason which I will share with you momentarily, I want you to know this man up close and personal.

Robert Williams began his spiritual saga at the age of 11 by walking down the aisle of the Pioneer Drive Baptist Church in Abilene, Texas, to "accept Jesus as his personal Lord and Savior." From there he "followed Jesus" through dozens of different churches in at least four denominations, to New Age study groups and gay religious caucuses, and finally into "high church" Anglo-Catholic worship. You may have read about him in conjunction with his ground-breaking place in history as the first openly gay priest to be ordained in the Episcopal Church.

The ordination took place under the auspices of Williams' mentor, the controversial John Spong, bishop of the Diocese of Newark, who was once quoted as saying that if the church could bless the hounds at a fox hunt, it could bless committed same-sex couples![28] But not even bishop Spong could keep back the hounds in the church and media when Williams suggested in a forum on celibacy that Mother Teresa's life would be greatly enhanced if she "got laid." Spong himself turned out the light in Williams' priestly office!

However, you should not dismiss Williams as a nut case. His understanding of Christian theology is as deep as it is perverse. At times his book is uncannily perceptive, and even profoundly spiritual—perhaps owing to the fact that he has been diagnosed as having AIDS, and is therefore forced to struggle with life's meaning.

His is not the only book written on pro-gay theology. Indeed, I have rummaged through a long shelf-full of such books. But none is more personal, and thus revealing, of the mind of one who is *convinced* that he is doing God's bidding as a practicing, proud, and—in his own words—"queer Christian."

A Struggle of Conscience

And that brings me to the point I want to make about not just Robert Williams but millions of gays whom I think he represents: *The gay-rights movement is aimed primarily at gaining public legitimacy for the homosexual lifestyle.* Not just legalization, but *legitimacy*. Yet there is another process going on behind the scenes that is far more personal: *a struggle of individual consciences.*

Let me go back to the questions I asked earlier: Why all the pretense at scholarly debate over the meaning of individual biblical passages? Why even bother opening the Bible in the first place? The answers to both of these questions, I propose, is that homosexual men and women *have* to deal with the Bible! Intuitively, they *know* that what they are doing is wrong, and they can't live with it.

Sadly for many homosexuals, they literally can't live with their consciences and tragically end up among the deplorable suicide statistics that haunt the nation's gays. Facile attempts to put the blame for their deaths on an unaccepting homophobic society only serve to perpetuate the problem.

Those who do not choose "the easy way out" are left to struggle within themselves. I suspect that the guilt is overwhelming. (It can be bad enough for heterosexual sin!) And that very guilt is the strongest experiential evidence possible that homosexuality is neither natural (in terms of what God intended) nor morally acceptable when acted upon (in terms of what God demands).

Longing for Acceptance

But it's not always just the guilt, and that brings me back to Robert Williams. He would probably deny it (he's far too feisty to beg sympathy), but laced throughout his book are what seem to be telltale cries for help, subtle pleas for love he never received, and a desperate longing for acceptance—from family, friends, the church, and most of all, his God.

Just catch the tone of these snippets strewn through his book:

> [Said by a friend,] "You are a very angry young man."[29]
>
> Chances are you grew up believing in a God who did not truly love you. A God who—like your human parents, perhaps—was disappointed in you, ashamed of you.[30]
>
> The person in my life who has consistently offered me the closest thing I have ever experienced to truly unconditional love is not my father or mother or lover, but my grandmother.[31]
>
> While my father seemed to be always working, and my mother was often too busy with her own work, I can't remember Grannie ever telling me not to bother her.[32]
>
> For many of us, it is difficult if not impossible to imagine our fathers ever saying to us, "You are my beloved child. I am proud of you."[33]
>
> Pride, far from being a sin for queers, is the remedy against sin. Our greatest sin is self-hatred, self-denigration. . . .[34]
>
> [Of his first visit to a gay bar,] Suddenly, this twenty-three-year-old man who had grown up feeling like an outcast, a sissy, felt affirmed, attractive, *wanted*.[35]

Am I reading too much into these statements, or has Robert Williams just told us how innocent babies grow up to be homosexuals? How different might Robert's life have been if his father had not always been working, and his mother not so busy with her own work? What if his father had said to him, "Son, I love you. I am proud of you"? What if from an early age Robert could have sung "Jesus Loves Me" with real confidence that it was truly so?

Somehow I have to believe that there might have been one less pro-gay theologian out there doing scholastic flip-flops in order to find a God who might accept him *just as he is.*

People don't just intentionally set out to go Bible-bashing. Behind every feminist and gay theologian is likely to be some early relationship gone terribly wrong. How many more "rebellious gay activists" are there out there, trying desperately to overcome their upbringing and somehow connect with God? And how many precious little ones are there in homes across America today, even in *Christian* homes, who one day will grow up fearing what the Bible teaches so much that they are willing to trash it, if necessary, to get some misguided sense of God's acceptance?

> *Jesus said, "Let the little children come to me, and do not hinder them, for the kingdom of heaven belongs to such as these."*[36]
>
> *But if anyone causes one of these little ones who believe in me to sin, it would be better for him to have a large millstone hung around his neck and to be drowned in the depths of the sea.*
>
> *"Woe to the world because of the things that cause people to sin! Such things must come, but woe to the man through whom they come!*[37]

CHAPTER 10

Will the Church Sell Out?

The church belongs to God and not to man; the church cannot become a tool of any social order.
—Samuel Moffett

Dear church deacons:

Last week, Tom Merrill and Bill Danforth came to my office inviting me to officiate at the blessing of their same-gender union (called the Blessing of Holy Union).

Tom Merrill, who plans to complete his doctoral studies in biology in the spring, has been a member of this congregation for five years. Bill Danforth is a Methodist who attends church here with Tom from time to time. They are requesting that the service be held in our sanctuary.

I have counseled with them for three sessions and am satisfied that the motivation for their request as well as their commitment to God, the church, and each other warrant a positive response. In spite of the complexity and controversial nature of their request, I feel led by my best understanding to serve as pastor at such a ceremony of blessing and commitment.

As elected leaders of the congregation, your
response is crucial to my judgement to proceed. I want you to share with me the responsibility of seeking the mind of Christ in this
matter.

Faithfully yours,

Pastor John Robinson

The gay movement will never succeed without the
help of the church. Without the blessing of the church, it
can never take the moral high ground. The question is:
Will the church sell out?

The letter presented above is a slightly altered version
of an actual letter which, completely unsolicited, has
ended up on my desk. Naturally, I have changed the
names to ensure anonymity. What I will disclose is that
the letter was written by a Baptist minister. I say this to
highlight the fact that the letter should not automatically
be associated with the denominations which have been
in the forefront of debate over the status of homosexuals.

In addition to the letter, I also received the text of two
sermons apparently preached by the same minister in
the years leading up to the controversial issue of whether
the ceremony of blessing should be performed. Because I
have heard most of the points made in a number of other
contexts, I have chosen to interact with those sermons in
this chapter so you can get some feel for what is beginning to happen in churches all across America.

What I hope to demonstrate is the subtlety—sometimes as thin as a communion wafer—being used by
church leaders to justify not only same-gender "marriages" but homosexual relations in general. Well-mean-
ing, Christ-centered believers are being taken in by the
subtlety, often against their strong biblical instincts to
the contrary.

Is Sexual Orientation a Gift of God?

In one of his sermons the pastor encouraged his flock to say "Yes" to the gift of sexuality, as the *embodied* grace of God. According to the pastor, this special grace includes the gift of our sexual bodies, the gift of our sensual and sexual feelings, and—the main point of his sermon—the gift of our sexual orientation. Let me quote from this point forward:

> By orientation I mean the direction of our sexual feelings. Is the direction primarily toward someone of the same sex or opposite sex?
> Let me frame what I regard to be a crucial question: Is a person's basic sexual orientation given and thereby discovered or is it chosen? Specifically, does a person choose to be homosexual, or discover himself or herself to be homosexual? Most research and informed opinion concludes—and it's my conclusion—that one's basic sexual orientation is constitutionally given and cannot be changed at will. Behavior can be changed and managed by will power; one's essential sexual preference cannot.

If it sounds as if the pastor is parroting what we have already discussed in this book regarding the crucial distinction between orientation and behavior, then we've already missed the subtlety. To say that one has a particular sexual orientation by some early age in his or her life is not the same as saying "one's basic sexual orientation is *constitutionally given* and cannot be changed at will." What he really means becomes obvious as we read the next sentence:

> If true, how cruel of the church to judge as an "abomination" what God has given in the creation of a person.

Of course, the Bible never once identifies *orientation* as an "abomination," only *behavior*. But that is not the crucial issue. Is the pastor really telling us that God *created* homosexuals *as* homosexuals? (Theories of "genetic" gayness are starting to look wonderfully benign!)

No thought could be more devastating in its myriad implications: *Did God really create homosexuals as homosexuals?*

The conclusion reached here is fatally flawed in two significant ways: First, if what we are discussing is "orientation" (as I take it to be his intent), then we would be saying that God *intended* one's homosexual orientation *as a gift of his creation*. This is the most serious misunderstanding of the day. To say that a person's sexual orientation is not necessarily of his or her own choosing is a quantum leap away from saying, on the other hand, that it is a gift from God.

Quite to the contrary, the Bible teaches us that God created woman as a suitable partner for man, and man for woman. It was never God's intention that one's sexual orientation would be directed toward those of his or her own gender. In light of the joyful celebration of the diversity of gender in Creation, it is total nonsense to say so.

Homosexual orientation can only be a product of the Fall. Somewhere along the line it is the result of sin. Perhaps gays are right, for example, in pointing to the sin of bullying and taunting. Even more likely is the sin of broken relationships; or abandonment of biblically ordained gender roles and responsibilities in the home; or perhaps physical and verbal abuse.

One thing you can count on: God does not give the "gift" of homosexuality. Jesus himself explodes that theory:

> Which of you, if his son asks for bread, will give him a stone? Or if he asks for a fish, will give him a snake?

> If you, then, though you are evil, know how
> to give good gifts to your children, how much
> more will your Father in heaven give good gifts
> to those who ask him![1]

No one even slightly familiar with the struggles associated with homosexuality can pretend that it could ever be a *good* gift! It's a blasphemy to even suggest it. The Father gives only good gifts.

Second, if the term "homosexual" is meant to include actual sexual behavior, then we would be placing blame on God for even biblically prohibited behavior. Although in later references the pastor pays lips service to the "sin" of homosexual behavior, even here he waffles on it so badly that his flock must surely have been left wondering:

> How cruel of God to allow some to be inherently homosexual, yet condemn any acknowledgement and responsible, caring expression of that gift.

Make no mistake about it, his point is that one's orientation acts as an *entitlement* to expression of that orientation. (Otherwise, why bless same-gender couples who obviously intend to have homosexual relations?)

As for the implied cruelty on God's part in the event that homosexual behavior is deemed to be sinful, is it any more cruel than for God to allow others to be inherently *heterosexual*, yet nevertheless expect them to refrain from biblically forbidden sex?

That's the trouble we get into if we accept the premise that *homosexual orientation itself* is a gift from God. We must then begin to do some fancy footwork to avoid the obvious teaching of Scripture regarding prohibited sexual behavior.

The Classic Cultural Arguments

From gay theologians, we have already had a preview of some of the cultural arguments which follow in the pastor's second sermon. But it is important to see how the cultural argument is made simultaneously in two opposite directions. In the first direction (cultural *irrelevance*), we are told that Scripture itself was fashioned out of cultural expectations of another era, and is therefore suspect. In the second direction (cultural *relevance*), we are told that current culture invites us to respond differently to whatever biblical teaching we might encounter.

We see the cultural *irrelevance* argument when the minister says:

> To be homosexual constitutionally is a rather recent understanding. The biblical writers assumed that everyone was basically heterosexual. So, of course, any homosexual acts would be viewed as totally "unnatural," going against the grain of creation.

Are we to believe that the Holy Spirit who "guided the apostles into all the truth"[2] was unaware of something that modern psychology has just now discovered? This argument says more about the pastor's dim view of divine revelation than his misunderstanding of any given passage. Apparently he disagrees with Paul, not only about homosexual sin, but Paul's assertion that "all Scripture is God-breathed and is useful for teaching, rebuking, correcting and training in righteousness, so that the man of God may be thoroughly equipped for every good work."[3]

It's no wonder, then, that we next hear the pastor saying:

> The Bible, when referring to homosexual acts, condemns them as expressions of lust and

pagan idolatry. In other words, exploitative, impersonal, self-centered, promiscuous sexual acts—whether heterosexual or homosexual—are condemned as wrong.

The implication, of course, is that nonexploitative, personal, loving, committed homosexual relations are *not* sinful. The same, apparently, goes for sex between heterosexuals outside of marriage, as long as it is shared with a "significant other." Of course, it would have been nice if the biblical writers could just have spelled out those details a bit more for us instead of leaving us to think foolishly that the words *fornication* and *sodomy* applied to *all* circumstances. They certainly don't *mention* any exceptions!

Apparently with a straight face, the minister says further,

> For good reason we are alarmed about the promiscuous activity of many homosexuals. But so are responsible gays!

Now we are being asked to identify and affirm "*responsible* gays." Would that be the same as "responsible murderers" who are alarmed about serial killers? (No, I don't equate homosexuals and murderers—only the logic.)

With his reference to "pagan idolatry" (as being the essence of the prohibition in Deuteronomy 23:17,18 rather than the homosexual prostitution which was involved), the pastor alerts us to the fact that he is in bed with gay theologians who notoriously abuse the context of specific passages in order to come up with tortured interpretations which manage to avoid the obvious meaning in light of the overall body of Scriptures which treat the subject.

Unfortunately, this and other pro-gay interpretation of specific biblical passages (as indicated in the previous chapter) is becoming more and more widespread. It's hard to tell whether gay activists are being indoctrinated by liberal theologians or whether liberal theologians are merely pandering to the pressure of the gay movement. In the pastor's case, at least one of his sermons was prompted by an anonymous letter from some "familiar stranger" (as it was signed) who asked, "Is 'abomination' the final word? I await your sermon next Sunday in hope and terror."

His question ("Is 'abomination' the final word?") is a compelling question for the cultural church today. In fact, it is the crucial issue of our time: *Is God's revealed Word the* **final** *word on whatever issue might arise?* Today's feminists, gays, and liberal theologians and pastors in the church are answering with a resounding "No!"

The Argument from Silence

Let's face it—it's very difficult to avoid the plain teaching of Scripture on the subject of homosexual behavior. Only a circus contortionist could have any hope of doing it. What then are the biblical options for those who are intent on circumventing the obvious? A classic response has been to make something out of nothing—that is, to read into the *silence* of Scripture whatever it is that one wishes to believe. When there are barriers set up in the road ahead, take to the open fields!

Our pastor provides us a good illustration of this hermeneutical maneuver:

> Neither does the Bible say anything one way or another about longterm, committed, caring homosexual relationships. Again, there is silence on that possibility.

Has it never occurred to the pastor that the reason why the Bible is silent on "respectable" homosexual relationships is because, by virtue of what the Bible *does* say, there *are no* "respectable" homosexual relationships? As previously, I am tempted to point out how untenable that argument is when you compare it with the implications for "respectable," if illicit, *heterosexual* relationships. Unfortunately, I have the feeling that the pastor would find nothing wrong with those relationships either!

But the most popular argument from silence (on any number of issues facing today's church) is yet to come:

> Jesus, our most authoritative biblical Word, says nothing about homosexuality, unless his respectful inference about the eunuch is considered (Matthew 19:1-12).

Just how shallow can our theology get? Is biblical authority to be nothing more than, If Jesus *didn't* mention something, it must be okay? Need I parade out the long list of things that Jesus *didn't* mention that, by such reasoning, would be morally acceptable? How about abortion and euthanasia? (No, sorry, those too are being justified in exactly the same way.) Then try these: rape, spousal abuse, genocide, bestiality, necrophilia, kidnapping, torture, burglary, gambling, drugs, prostitution, auto theft, computer fraud. . . . Need I go on? On these specific topics and more, Jesus said not a word.

If you knew me really well, you would know how ironic it is that I should be contesting an "argument from silence." I have just written a whole chapter in another book[4] extolling the use of "argument by silence"—but, importantly, only when the context clearly indicates that the silence was *specifically intended* to convey some spiritual principle or teaching.

Gratuitously listening for Simon-and-Garfunkel-type "sounds of silence" can leave us hearing virtually anything we want to hear. Before that happens, we need to listen again to the words of Habakkuk when he reminds us that "the LORD is in his holy temple; let all the earth be silent before him."[5]

As for Matthew 19:1-12, the pastor was far too dismissive. Perhaps Jesus *did* address at least one aspect of homosexuality—in fact, the very issue at hand: What is a Christian to do if he has homosexual leanings?

In that passage, Jesus had just delivered to the religious leaders some hard teaching on marriage, divorce, and remarriage. They didn't like what they heard. Even Jesus' disciples were disturbed by its implications and, once away from the Pharisees, opined: "If this is the situation between a husband and wife, it is better not to marry."

Jesus' response was to affirm that, indeed, there are circumstances under which we must all make some difficult choices "because of the kingdom of heaven." For one Christian, being in the kingdom may mean not divorcing and remarrying, even when present marital circumstances would seem to encourage it. For another, it may mean the formidable prospect of remaining sexually pure until marriage, even if that means a lifetime of celibacy.

For the person who struggles with his or her homosexuality, being in the kingdom clearly means renouncing any physical expression of those feelings. Such strugglers, perhaps more than anyone, will know what it means to be a "eunuch because of the kingdom of heaven."

"Everything's Up-to-Date in Kansas City"

The pastor's second sermon also provides us with the perfect transitional statement, as we move from cultural *irrelevance* to cultural *relevance*. Indeed, the two are always found in tandem, because when you discard the old paradigm, you must replace it with the new:

We can be oppressed, held down, held back,
by *cultural values presented as ultimate truth*.

Indeed, the task of the Christian maturation is to sort out learned morals, assessing which ones fit our current understanding of life and the life of Christ. Through the fabric of socialization we seek to hear the voice and will of God.

Nothing is more frightening to the postmodern culture today than those words—dare I repeat them—*ultimate truth*. This is the "If-it-feels-good-believe-it" generation of moral relativity and tolerance. In the church, "if it feels good, *sanctify* it!"

But look closely. Neither the pastor nor any of the new wave of liberation theologians ever comes right out and denies the existence of ultimate truth. That would give away the game. They simply employ the subtle twist which says, What we are presented in the Bible is as likely to be man's disposable cultural values as God's ultimate truth.

Suppose for a moment that they are right. How then will we know the difference between ultimate truth and mere cultural baggage in the Bible? The answer comes back, It's a matter of "our understanding" looking "through the fabric of socialization." In other words, we see truth in whatever way current culture has trained our eye to see it. "The fabric of socialization" is just another way of saying that we are using "cultural lenses." Instead of looking at the Bible first, and then applying what we read to current culture, we begin by looking at current culture and reading its standards and values back *into* the Bible.

The upshot of such a process is the elevation of culture over Scripture, of man over God. And what happens to *ultimate truth* along the way? In the Church of What's Happening Now, it is sanctimoniously sacrificed to the gods of faddishness, expediency, and social pressure.

Because Paul's inspired writings themselves are so discredited by the very process we are discussing, one wonders whether they will still carry any weight. But if anyone in the church is still listening, this problem of cultural relevance is exactly what Paul was describing for us in Romans 1 when he charged that there were those who had "exchanged the truth of God for a lie, and worshiped and served created things rather than the Creator."[6]

And who are the "they" he is talking about? Among others, the very ones we are talking about: *homosexuals*. Of this same passage and the sin it denounces, the pastor says:

> This lustful act of homosexuality is denounced but it is not singled out for special attention.

To the contrary, Paul did in fact single out homosexual behavior as the premier badge of ungodliness, just as Jude did in his own epistle. You simply cannot rationalize something as obviously immoral as homosexual behavior without exchanging the truth of God for a lie, and elevating man and his perceived "needs" over the Word of God, which was "*once for all* entrusted to the saints."[7]

In the Beginning...

The sad irony of the sermons which this pastor presented is that he hurriedly skipped right over the key to the whole issue. In attempting to justify performing the Blessing of Holy Union for Tom and Bill, the pastor referred, without further comment, to "sex and covenant love—what God has joined together let not man or woman put asunder." It was one last, desperate attempt to justify the unjustifiable—to suggest that whatever is unholy can be made holy simply by introducing the concept of "covenant" with its biblical ring.

But those very words of Jesus which the pastor referenced[8] should alone settle the entire issue. All we need to do is to see who it was that God joined together. It was, of course, one *man* and one *woman*. Failing to see what was staring him in the face all along, the pastor was prepared to do on behalf of God what not even the law in his state was willing to officially recognize: the joining together of man with man, or woman with woman.

"What God has joined together, let no man put asunder" ought to be a sober warning to the church: What God has *not* joined together, man *must* keep asunder.

Close Calls and Near Misses

Just in case you somehow missed the recent brouhaha among Presbyterians over sexual ethics, it was one of the great religious stirs of the decade, spawned when the church's Special Committee on Human Sexuality recommended the adoption of the following resolutions:

> That "all persons, whether heterosexual or homosexual, whether single or partnered, have a moral right to experience justice-love in their lives and to be sexual persons."
>
> That gays and lesbians be received as full participant members, and for ordination, "regardless of their sexual orientation."
>
> That worship resources be designed to celebrate same-sex relationships.
>
> That the problem before the church is not sexual sin but the "prevailing social, cultural, and ecclesial arrangements...[and] conformity to the unjust norm of compulsory heterosexuality."[9]

The committee attempted to justify the above resolutions by saying, "A reformation of sexual ethics is called for precisely because social conditions have changed."

Here in tangible form was the end product of pro-gay and cultural theology. It was no longer just idle talk about biblical teaching on the subject of sexual ethics. This was a calculated pro-gay assault on a major denomination.

When the time came for the General Assembly to vote on the committee's proposals, at least some sense of sanity prevailed: The vote was 534 to 31 against. Some 86 of the denomination's 171 presbyteries sent "overtures" to the General Assembly, all but one denouncing the committee's report.[10]

In a Pastoral Letter to be read in all 11,505 Presbyterian churches the following Sunday, the Assembly said, "We continue to abide by the 1978 and 1979 positions of the Presbyterian Church on homosexuality," which included the following excerpts:

> We conclude that homosexuality is not God's wish for humanity. . . .
> Christians are responsible to view their sins as God views them and strive against them. To evade this responsibility is to permit the church to model for the world forms of sexual behavior that may seriously injure individuals, families. . . .
> We believe Jesus Christ intends the ordination of officers to be a sign of hope. . . . Therefore our present understanding of God's will precludes the ordination of persons who do not repent of homosexual practice.[11]

Given the landslide vote against the unprecedented assault on moral decency within the Presbyterian church, the outcome was not exactly a near-miss. But it is chilling enough to think that the report got as far as it did, or even surfaced at all! What it ought to tell the Christian community is that it takes only a few well-placed pro-gay activists to make serious inroads into the church.

Tempest over a Prayer Book

Living in England for several months each year, I can report that the Church of England is still holding out against gay activists—so far. When the Labour Party in the last campaign yielded to gay activists on lowering the age of homosexual consent to 16, Labour's plan split the church, already divided over homosexual rights. The Lesbian and Gay Christian movement, which claims more than 4000 members, expressed its delight that Labour had "seen sense" on the age of consent. Working parties within the church have recommended that consideration be given to blessing gay relationships and supporting the adoption and fostering of children by gay or lesbian couples.

The latest volley in the escalating war with gay activists was fired when the Society for the Promotion of Christian Knowledge (SPCK) announced that it would be publishing *Daring to Speak Love's Name, A Gay and Lesbian Prayer Book*. The announcement caused an explosion of hostility and revulsion, leading George Carey, Archbishop of Canterbury, to threaten resignation of the presidency of SPCK. Naturally, his bold action was immediately met with cries of "homophobia" and "censorship."

What was the subject of this homophobic censorship? Here is a brief excerpt from the Rite of Repentance:

> "And the serving girl, on seeing him, said to the bystanders: This Man is one of them. But again he denied it."
>
> We remember those times when we have denied that we were "one of them". The times when we have smiled at and even joined in the anti-gay jokes for fear of being exposed as "one of them". The times when we have betrayed

> God our creator, ourselves and our gay broth-
> ers and sisters by denying implicitly or explic-
> itly that we are "one of them".[12]

A secular publisher has now stepped in and printed the prayer book. While leading clerics have condemned it as blasphemous, other bishops praised it as "a genu-inely useful piece of work." The all-things-to-all-people Bishop of Durham, David Jenkins, provided a foreword.

Regarding the controversial book, the Bishop of Edin-burgh, Richard Holloway, commented: "It is inappro-priate to cling to a prejudice that dates from the mythical destruction of Sodom in the prehistoric era...."[13] How does one begin to respond to someone who ought to know better?

The Church of England has recently succumbed to pressure from women's groups and approved the ordi-nation of women priests. Only time will tell whether the pressure on the Church from gay activists will push it over the brink on this issue as well. It is important to remember that events in England are not unconnected with the Anglican community worldwide. Any inroad on one side of the Atlantic is likely to be felt on the other side as well.

Women Opening Doors for Gays

More important than what might happen in the Church of England or in the larger Anglican community is the connection between the already-accomplished ordina-tion of women as priests and now the call for ordination of gay priests. Theologically, the path to one doesn't exactly lead directly to the other (the gender of priests is not a matter of morality, as is homosexual behavior), but hermeneutically it's a straight line.

I have yet to see an argument put forward on behalf of

gays that I haven't already seen successfully used in promoting a wider role for women in the church. Principally, of course, it is the cultural argument ("How can we trust Scriptures arising out of a first-century patriarchal culture?"). But, sounding far more respectable, the arguments are also based on calls for a Christ-centered approach ("What would Jesus do today?") or appeals to "justice-love" ("What do love and justice require of us?").

Despite their compelling facade, the latter two questions move us away from an *objective* search for truth into the realm of *subjective* evaluations. When Scripture is viewed subjectively, Jesus has a strange way of always doing precisely what *we* would do. When objective biblical study is abandoned, "justice-love" has a peculiar way of being whatever the latest politically-correct party line would dictate.

The church is fooling itself if it thinks it can open the door to feminist theology without gays sticking their foot through the same doorway. When you undermine the authority of Scripture in order to resolve any one particular issue, you undermine it on every front. Credibility has a domino effect: Push the first one over, and they all fall down. Today it's women's role (a matter of doctrine); tomorrow it's gay liberation (a matter of morality). If we can't trust Paul regarding women, how can we trust him regarding gays?

Selling out to the gay movement, should that happen, will come at a high price. In the church today, we are facing the very real prospect of abandoning altogether our commitment to biblical authority. And if that is where we are headed, then we might as well go ahead now and turn out the lights. At that point, Sodom's second coming will have been complete.

The Dangerous Fifth Column

In the spirit of candor, there is a final concern that

simply has to be aired. I'm afraid that the most dangerous enemy is not some amorphous gay movement "out there" somewhere among the secular humanists who are behind the current assault. Where the church is most vulnerable is from *within*. And here I am no longer talking about doctrine or hermeneutics or biblical authority. I'm talking about the gay fifth column which is already in the church.

If you are not familiar with the term *fifth column*, it was first used back in 1936 when the forces of Francisco Franco rose up against the Spanish republic. One of Franco's top officers, General Mola, had besieged Madrid from the outside with four columns of soldiers. In addition, he boasted of having a "fifth column" within —those people in Madrid who were giving aid and support to Franco's forces. It was no idle boast. With the help of the "fifth column," Franco's forces were able to achieve the victory.

In the church today the fifth column is already in place, and its ranks are swelling with each day that passes. It's the growing number of gay clergy we're talking about here. I don't for one minute buy the "10 percent gay" propaganda as it relates to the general population. But the incidence of gays may indeed be significant among the clergy in some churches.

Fear of reprisals keeps virtually all gay clergy "closeted," but pro-gay polls in the United States have suggested that around 25 percent of Episcopal priests and 50 percent of Roman Catholic priests are gay. A recent study of the Church of England reported that 15 to 30 percent of their priests are gay.[14] Because these figures come through pro-gay sources, they undoubtedly need to be significantly downsized. Nevertheless, there can be no question but that the figures are high.

Anecdotally, former gay priest Robert Williams says:

Nor is the phenomenon limited to the liturgical churches (although we do have a penchant for smells and bells, not to mention lacy vestments!). I had a friend who was the organist in a large Southern Baptist church in Texas, and he was part of a large network of highly closeted but highly active gay Southern Baptist clergy and musicians. The image of the priest performing the marriage ceremony at the end of *La Cage aux Folles*, prissily turning the page of the prayer book, is indelibly printed in our memory because it is such a common archetype.[15]

Whatever the actual number of gays in the ministry, it is enough to spawn the running joke among gay clergy:

Q: How many straight priests does it take to screw in a light bulb?

A: Both of them.

Rightly or wrongly, there has always been suspicion of homosexual activity among priests who have taken vows of celibacy. To whatever extent this suspicion may be true, it is an unnecessary occupational hazard tragically caused by faulty, nonbiblical doctrine. ("The Spirit clearly says that in later times some will abandon the faith. . . . They forbid people to marry. . . .)[16]

But doctrinal celibacy aside, by its very nature religion as a vocation tends to attract those who are softer and more sensitive. Homosexuals are often found in nurturing roles both inside and outside the church. Some gays suggest that their priesthood is an extension of the more ancient shamans, who were mediators between the tribe and the realm of the spirit. These shamans, or berdaches, were said to be "not man/not woman," but mediators between masculine and feminine traits and thus suited to their role as mediators between the spiritual and the mundane.[17]

One also wonders how many gays are attracted to the ministry as an avenue through which to deal with the guilt associated with homosexual behavior. Is the priesthood seen as penance? Or perhaps a perceived bulwark against the lusts by which one is bedeviled?

If there is any radical change taking place in the clergy today, it is the influx of feminists. Seminaries are churning out women theologians at the same or higher rate as business schools and law schools. And, as we have already seen, one can never discount the feminist/gay connection. How would one ever know what percentage of radical feminist/lesbians are among the legions of women now entering the clergy?

Robert Williams points, for example, to Episcopal Divinity School in Cambridge, Massachusetts. "EDS," he says, "happens to be one of the most politically and theologically progressive seminaries in the world, as well as a leading center of feminist theology and a very gay-positive environment. . . . After one semester, I came to realize that feminist Christian concerns and gay Christian concerns are, at root, the same."[18]

What all of this amounts to is a time bomb waiting to go off. When the circumstances are ripe, the fifth column is going to raise its ugly head and the church will easily succumb from within. All it takes is a critical mass of gay clergy to sway the entire church.

In the meantime, we are already facing the potential for compromise. How likely is it that a church influenced by its gay clergy is going to speak out boldly on the issue of gay rights? And if the clergy doesn't speak out, who will?

The prospects are too horrendous to contemplate. Without vociferous protest from the clergy, there will not be protest from the church. Without protest from the church, there will not be protest from society. Without protest from society, gayness will become acceptable. When gayness becomes acceptable, there will no longer be any need for gay clergy to be closeted. And when that happens—call me an alarmist if you wish—just how far removed will we be (in what is already a neopagan, post-Christian society) from the homosexual shrine prostitutes of Deuteronomy 23?

Reason for Concern?

I hope I'm not reading too much into Archbishop Roger Mahony's recent conditional acceptance of gays in the military.[19] In earlier rounds against gay activists, the Los Angeles archbishop has stood firm. But his contradiction of Archbishop Joseph T. Dimino, the U.S. Roman Catholic Church's highest-ranking military prelate, suggests signs of fissure within the church on the question of gays.

The Mahony blip aside, will the Catholic Church remain as stalwart against gay rights as it has against abortion? Is there any reason to fear that a fifth column in the Catholic Church weakens its power to respond with the same courage and conviction?

So far, Church leaders like Cardinal O'Connor and Cardinal Law have been stalwarts in the fight. The Christian community needs to pray that these and other church leaders, both Catholic and non-Catholic, throughout the nation can continue to have a positive influence on the younger priests, pastors, and evangelists, who, whether gay or not gay, are products of a culture that has all but received the final payment in selling out to the gays.

Jesus was definitely *not* gay, as some people blasphemously allege. But there are many Judases within the church today who clearly are. And many more who, though not gay themselves, are prepared to offer up the 30 pieces of silver in the form of wrongheaded pro-gay theology. God save us from the gay movement without, but most of all from the enemy within.

CHAPTER 11

Storming the Courts for Gay Rights

I don't know why gays want to be in the armed forces. They seem to look for something they're denied and then insist on having it.

—Quentin Crisp, gay
activist and author

In Atlanta in 1982, 29-year-old Michael Hardwick was cited by the police for carrying an open bottle of liquor in public. After he failed to answer the summons, a bench warrant was issued for his arrest. When the officer went to Hardwick's house to serve the warrant, he happened to observe through a partly opened bedroom door that Hardwick and another man were engaged in an act of fellatio. An arrest followed, and Hardwick was charged with sodomy under a Georgia statute with a maximum 20-year penalty. The statute's reference to oral and anal sex made no distinction between homosexuals and heterosexuals. (Only four states do.)

Hardwick immediately challenged the arrest, alleging violation of his rights to privacy and due process. The district attorney refused to submit the case to the grand jury, in effect dismissing the charges. (There had been no criminal prosecutions under the statute for decades.) However, sensing the opportunity for a test case, Hardwick pressed for a declaratory judgment, hoping to have the Georgia statute declared unconstitutional. Appeals went all the way to the U.S. Supreme Court, where in 1986 *Bowers v. Hardwick* became a landmark case.[1]

The significance of the case was summarized by Illinois law professor Gerard V. Bradley: "Hardwick's predicament was ideally suited to serve as a referendum on what for his generation was a pivotal legal question, namely, must the state remain 'neutral' on questions of the morally good life, and stay its hand until 'harm' to innocent bystanders is threatened? Put another way: since the 'neutrality' and 'harm' principles are the distinguishing features of philosophical liberalism, the issue is, are our institutions to be determined by liberal political morality?"[2]

In a closely contested five-to-four decision, the Court held the Georgia statute constitutional—at least with reference to *homosexual* sodomy. (Since it was a gay person who challenged the law, the Court said he had a right to question the statute only as it might apply to gays.) When the majority expressed doubt in a footnote as to whether the statute would be constitutional if applied to *heterosexuals*, the perceived double standard naturally brought howls of protest from gay activists.

Constitutionally, the Court said that no "fundamental right" under due process was effectively raised by Hardwick, and that therefore Georgia did not have to prove some "compelling state interest" in order to justify prohibiting homosexual behavior among its citizens. All the state needed to prove was some rational basis for the prohibition, and that was provided by the public's historic disapproval of such behavior. (As recently as 1961, *all* states had such statutes.)

The effect of the ruling, then, was to say that homosexual relations between consenting adults, even in the privacy of their own bedrooms, could be made criminal by state statutes.

The majority's decision was not terribly artful, undoubtedly owing to the Court's continual unease with how to handle moral issues. Nevertheless, they managed in their own bungling secular way to reach the right conclusion. (Because sodomy laws were on the books at the time the Constitution was adopted, the original framers of the Constitution undoubtedly would be shocked to learn that anyone today dared suggest that sodomy laws were unconstitutional!)

There was an interesting historical footnote to *Hardwick*. Justice Lewis Powell changed his vote during the writing stage to join with the majority. After he retired from the bench, Powell told a Harvard Law School gathering that changing his mind was the biggest mistake he had made as a Justice. Gays in the audience were poised in jubilation until Powell added the tag: "but it hardly matters"!

Hardwick was a high-stakes game. Gays were less interested in *winning* (relative to laws which are rarely enforced anyway) than in *setting a precedent*. It wasn't *criminal* discrimination that the gays were targeting, but *civil* discrimination.

What they wanted, but didn't get, in *Hardwick* was a ruling that would have elevated "sexual orientation" (as they have craftily worded it) to the status of a fundamental right. Had that happened, then 1) states could not have discriminated against gays in any area of the law unless they could show some *compelling* reason to do so; and 2) the effect would have been *permanent*. (Sympathetic Presidents may not always be around.)

Attempted Hijacking of Legitimate Status

In the area of Constitutional law, nothing is more important to gay activists than achieving a status reserved for minorities with "immutable traits," like race and gender. (That's what all the frantic efforts to find a "gay gene" are about. If it's *biological*, it must be *legal*!)

The key to being among the class of those receiving the highest level of review is whether a particular group historically has been subjected to unreasonable, stereo-typical classifications without any basis *in fact*. And it is crucial to remember that what is contemplated here is *official government policy and action*, not private discrimination or even gay-bashing by the most despicable homosexual-hating individual citizens.

Gays love to compare themselves with blacks and women, as if their histories and circumstances are parallel. (Interestingly, not even blacks and women are treated exactly the same Constitutionally.) But as compared to gays, there is one immediate difference: Blacks and women have been discriminated against not for what they *do* but simply for being who they *are*. Despite all the language of sexual "orientation," specifically designed to *sound like status*, the fact is that it is not "orientation" to which the public has objected for centuries on end, but to *conduct*. That is, and will always remain, the Achilles' heel of the gay argument.

To turn that issue around, the question is: Is there any reason to elevate homosexuals to the very highest level of legal protection simply because of their *lifestyle*? Would we ever do the same for the lifestyle of *heterosexuals*, married or unmarried? One's choices about sexual and marital conduct are just that—*choices*, not "immutable traits."

There is simply no basis in fact for alleging historical discrimination against homosexual "orientation," as such. And when orientation becomes *behavior*, then it is easily demonstrated that the special classification of homosexuals is *reasonable*, related as it is to moral character and whatever impact that may have on a given job or housing situation. Government action against homosexuals—as in sodomy laws—has always reflected society's values.

A further important factor in finding historical discrimination against a particular group of citizens is the inability of the group to fight back politically. Who can doubt that—even if they don't always get what they want—the gay movement is one of the most politically astute, highly financed, and tactically effective political action groups in America today! In fact, far from being politically disadvantaged, gay activists are so focused on a single issue that they run circles around the majority of citizens, who have more diffused agendas to think about.

In an article entitled "L.A.'s New Gay Muscle," *Los Angeles Times* writer Bettina Boxall quotes Duane Garrett, chairman of Dianne Feinstein's successful Senate campaign, as saying: "I don't believe that any politician seeking statewide support in either party would be foolish enough to ignore the potential support of the gay community. I think the days are gone when you can run . . . even for a nomination for the Republican Party, bashing gays and gay lifestyles."[3]

Former Los Angeles Mayor Tom Bradley said of all the gay political muscle flexing—and its recognition by mainstream politicos—that it is "a matter of the time being right."[4]

Addressing a group of gay and lesbian attorneys in Los Angeles, Senator Barbara Boxer agreed: "I could not have won my election without the support of the gay and lesbian community. Rest assured, I will not forget you and your issues." Boxall says, "Boxer's Hollywood campaign office sometimes felt like Gay Central."[5]

There is sweet irony in some of what is reported these days about the supposed woes of homosexuals both politically and economically. When word spread quickly about a California gubernatorial veto of a gay-rights measure (to be discussed in detail momentarily), Boxall writes: "To everyone's amazement, BMW professionals poured out of hangouts [to hit the streets in protest.] Attorney and activist Carol Anderson got off a plane from San Francisco and headed straight for the intersection of San Vicente and Santa Monica boulevards, where a crowd of about 250 was milling about. 'People were in tears, literally standing on the sidewalk crying, because they couldn't conceive that the governor would say we didn't have a right to work,' recalls Anderson. . . ."[6]

No right to work? Are gays seriously trying to tell us that attorneys and "BMW professionals" are out of work because they happen to prefer having sex with those of their own gender? That's the biggest farce since Ford said Pintos were safe! Gays are hardly a political or economic underclass. In fact, *USA Today* reports that "homosexual couples who live together may be wealthier than heterosexual live-in couples, an analysis of new Census numbers suggests." Experts say the findings suggest that "gay male couples appear to be particularly affluent, out-earning even married couples: Gay male couples had a $56,863 household income; Married couples, $47,012; Heterosexual unmarried couples, $37,602."[7]

In short, there is simply no *need* to elevate homosexuals to a class entitled to "fundamental rights" as that term is used in law. Considering that they comprise no more than 1 to 3 percent of the population, gays already have overrepresented and unprecedented political clout!

It wouldn't concern gay activists, I suppose, but the rest of us have to ask ourselves whether elevating homosexuals to a "suspect class" is really worth diluting the value we place on better-served causes like blacks and women. Inevitably, if less-than-genuine classes are put into the same category as genuine classes in need of legitimate protection, the time will come when that protection will have to be compromised in order to accommodate the lowest common denominator within the group.

Perhaps I can illustrate that concern by pointing to affirmative action laws which *require* the hiring of minorities so as to make up for past discriminatory policies.

However you may feel about affirmative action programs (they are under increasing attack), simply consider this very real possibility: If homosexuals were ever raised to the level of a "suspect class," the next logical step would be for them to demand that employers be *required* to hire a certain percentage of gays. (Don't think for a moment that this isn't in the game plan.)

If that demand for inverse discrimination on behalf of gays were deemed to be inappropriate, then it would tend to weaken the argument of those blacks who seek extraordinary relief by way of affirmative action. Whether or not the specific issue is affirmative action, the question is, Should blacks and women, who can't possibly change their *status*, be handicapped by being lumped together with homosexuals, who clearly have personal control over what they *do*?

That political maneuvering aside, gays making gains on the coattails of discrimination against blacks has its own risks for the gay movement. Could it be that gays are vulnerable to a charge of racial discrimination themselves? For example, there is this comment by Bettina Boxall: "L.A.'s gay politics in many ways remains chiefly the province of affluent Westsiders, more often male than female and mostly white."[8]

L.A. Council candidate Conrado Terrazas, himself a gay, observes of gay politics that "it's changing, but it's basically a white person's game." And Lambda's L.A. director, J. Craig Fong, agrees: "My feeling here in Los Angeles is that every time communities of color have wanted a place at the table, they have had to fight their way in."[9]

Those who scream loudly about discrimination and who trade self-righteously on the discrimination of others should be the last to be found guilty of the same sin.

Making a Statement

In *Hardwick*, both sides to the controversy were more interested in symbolism than fact. *Symbolism* explains why sodomy statutes remain on the books in 24 states, despite notorious lack of enforcement. These two dozen states waste little public resources playing Peeping Tom with homosexuals. Actual enforcement is not the point. More than anything, the statutes are intended as a statement of public disapproval. They are, if you will, legislated pronouncements of social taboos.

Before you conclude that having officially unenforced laws on the books is strange beyond belief, simply consider the so-called "statutory rape" laws found in all 50 states. Like sodomy laws, they too are rarely enforced. Nevertheless they stand as legal guardians of the sexual purity of underaged females. Do you know of any man who doesn't know the significance of "jail bait"? There are times when a law doesn't have to be strictly enforced in order to be effective.

To a lesser extent, we see the same principle in operation with gambling, prostitution, and "soft" drugs like marijuana. Due to the consensual nature of the activities, there is less enforcement than there otherwise might be. Even so, through its laws the public maintains the right to say, "We don't like it." And it's a perfectly legitimate use of the law.

What bothers gays about such legislated "moral pronouncements" is not just their perpetuation of public attitudes against homosexual behavior, but the spin-off implications for other laws. When gays insist that there should be no discrimination in hiring based upon homosexual behavior, any jurisdiction having sodomy laws can always say, "But you're asking us to hire potential *felons* to teach our children and to work in child-care centers. We wouldn't do that with anyone else regularly engaged in felonious activity!"

And we see the same arguments being made in the current controversy over gays in the military. Under current military law, sodomy is presently an offense. How then can the military accept among their forces men and women who openly acknowledge that they are in ongoing violation of military regulations? (It's no answer to say, "Well, then, why not just get rid of the regulation forbidding sodomy?" For the military, especially, there are defensible reasons why the prohibition is there in the first place, including privacy, discipline, potential HIV transmission, etc.)

What the gays recognize far better than we do is the tapestry effect—the interconnection of seemingly unconnected criminal and civil laws. When it comes to gays' Constitutional rights, or the lack of them at present, Lady Justice wears a robe made of seamless cloth. If *Hardwick* had been decided in their favor, gays could have pretty much won the day in a single stroke.

Choose Your Forum

Any good lawyer will tell you that just because you lose in one court doesn't mean the ball game is over. For the diligent counselor, it is "try, try, again!" And that is what gay activists are doing. In *Hardwick* they lost at the federal level. It would have made things far easier had they won, but—not to worry—there is always Plan B: establishing gay rights state by state, city council by city council. Each state, of course, has its own constitution, generally protecting rights of privacy and offering due process. It is to these constitutions that the gay movement has turned for protection.

Attempting to *amend* state constitutions to provide greater protection for gays means having to deal with the entire citizenry through some form of ballot measure. For obvious reasons, this has not been the method of choice for gays. Instead, they have sometimes turned to state *legislatures*. But because of similar political pressure from constituents back home, that approach has not often produced desired results.

That leaves the court system, where gays have been doing a brisk business. Courts have all the advantages of 1) having sympathetic ears (for the most part); 2) being generally outside the public eye; and 3) lacking political pressure from anti-gay public sentiment. The only disadvantage to gays is the risk that, if they ever lose, the precedent that is set is long-lasting and difficult to reverse.

It doesn't always take convincing either the state legislature or the courts. For example, in 1979 an executive order was issued by California Governor Edmund G. Brown (Jerry Brown's father) prohibiting discrimination on the basis of sexual orientation in state employment. This is gay rights by fiat—the easiest of all methods to pursue—but it is extremely limited in scope.

Each city, of course, has its own ordinances which can be successfully targeted by a relatively small group of gay activists with strong local political clout. City councils are inherently defenseless when it comes to staving off any kind of political activists; they are simply too vulnerable at the next election. The District of Columbia, a unique jurisdictional entity in itself, demonstrates the kind of results you can get at the local level. Its Human Rights Act (a virtual menagerie of civil rights, and special interests masquerading as civil rights) bans—

> discrimination including, but not limited to, discrimination by reason of race, color, religion, national origin, sex, age, marital status, personal appearance, sexual orientation, family responsibilities, matriculation, political affiliation, physical handicap, source of income and place of residence or business.

Whew! In case you're wondering, "personal appearance" refers to "bodily condition" and manner or style of dress. You'll be relieved to know that it does *not* preclude a "requirement of cleanliness." The young man behind the counter at McDonald's may be wearing a pink tutu, but you can be assured that it's been properly washed!

A similar local ordinance in Madison, Wisconsin, led to what can only be described as a nightmare scenario. When Ann Hacklander and Maureen Rowe advertised for a third roommate, one of the applicants, Cari Sprague, disclosed that she was a lesbian. Their refusal to share the apartment with Ms. Sprague landed them before the Madison Equal Opportunities Commission, which promptly required Ann and Maureen to apologize to Ms. Sprague and pay her 1500 dollars for emotional distress. To drive home their point, MEOC also monitored Ann and Maureen's living arrangements for two years, and required that they attend a sensitivity training class taught by homosexuals![10]

Under pressure, the city council later amended the law to exclude roommate situations. But in light of the gestapo tactics which had already taken place, does anyone still believe that the cry of "Sodom's second coming" is just so much fundamentalist fear-mongering?

Legal Gymnastics in an All-Gay Olympics

Despite many gains at the state and local levels, gays in California have often been politically frustrated. Until recently, gay-rights legislation had been vetoed when it reached the Governor's office. In 1991, Assembly Bill 101 would have amended the Fair Housing Act to add "sexual orientation" to the list of factors which could not be considered in providing housing and employment. By the time it got to the governor's desk, it had been politically pared down to prohibit only discrimination in employment.

Governor Pete Wilson infuriated gays with a surprise veto, saying that the legislation was not really necessary under existing protections, and, more importantly, "it would create a bad business climate for California."

That excuse was as phony to Christians as to gays. Although Christians were pleased with the result, if not the explanation for it, gay activists weren't at all happy. Prepared to dance in the streets, they rioted there instead! I'm not sure what other reaction Governor Wilson expected. During his campaign for office, he had wooed the gays with a promise of his undying love and support.

For gays, it was just another reminder that concerted public pressure from citizens who still have their sense of morality intact can thwart the best-laid plans of mice and other politicians. Yet they remained undaunted, and eventually Governor Wilson came through for California gays by signing a slightly modified version of the earlier AB-101.

That successful bit of gay-rights legislation, Assembly Bill 2601, first introduced in February 1992, was designed to codify an earlier (1979) case which was nothing if not ingenious in its reasoning. In *Gay Law Students Association v. Pacific Telephone and Telegraph Co.*,[11] the California Supreme Court faced the issue of whether a public utility could automatically exclude all homosexuals from consideration for employment. It was no surprise when the court ruled that the utility was covered under the California constitution's equal protection guarantee. The surprise came when the court drew from the California Labor Code, which prohibits employers from interfering with any *political activities* on the part of their employees.

Affirming an earlier decision, the court held that "political activity" includes the espousal of a cause and that "the struggle of the homosexual community for equal rights, particularly in the field of employment, must be recognized as a political activity." Therefore, no employer can discriminate against "manifest" homosexuals or against those who made "an issue of their homosexuality."

The scope of this case is incredibly broad, because *any* homosexual is a "manifest homosexual" if his identity as a homosexual is known. This ruling resulted in the ultimate gay marriage: a legally recognized union between homosexual behavior and free speech/political action.

In the wake of the *Gay Law Students* case, the California Attorney General issued an opinion that, if presented with the issue, the courts probably would "protect the employees from discrimination on the basis of *undisclosed* or *suspected* homosexual orientation in the same manner as they protect employees from discrimination on the basis of open homosexual identification."

The effect of the law that Governor Wilson signed was to extend the court's reasoning (including "actual or perceived sexual orientation") not just to public utilities but to all *private* employers who regularly hire five or more persons in their business. For obvious political purposes, nonprofit religious organizations are generally exempted. However, Christians who run "for-profit" businesses and who happen to employ more than five employees have no religious-grounds safeguard.

You can rest assured that the California result will not be isolated in its impact. (Seven other states—Wisconsin, Massachusetts, Connecticut, New Jersey, Vermont, Minnesota, and Hawaii—already have similar legislation relating to housing, employment, and education.) Stay tuned for whatever may be the latest innovative piece of legislation in whatever state you call home. Never underestimate the resolve—or creativity—of legal minds bent on gay mischief.

Of course, all the legal maneuvering in the world to make homosexual conduct a fundamental legal right is never going to be the sexy issue that will capture America's attention. It sounds too dull. What's guaranteed to hit the headlines and provide fodder for Donahue and Oprah is the issue of privacy. Don't we all have a *right of privacy*? What we are about to see in the next chapter is not just a legal issue for the courts to decide. The issue of privacy is nothing less than an all-out cultural war!

CHAPTER 12

It's an All-Out Cultural War

Why shouldn't two men be able to dance at Disneyland? If they're young and in love, what harm does it do?

—Leonard Graff, legal
director of National
Gay Rights Advocates

Would you want the government to tell you what you can and cannot do in the privacy of your own home? Then why do you feel it should be different for gays? It's a legitimate question. And as unlikely as it seems, it is the line of demarcation between two opposing forces engaged in a far-flung cultural war.

Despite the rhetoric, the "privacy" we're talking about in terms of gay rights has little to do with bathhouses and bedrooms. First, because what goes on there is almost never the subject of government interference. Second, because there is no *absolute* right of privacy in *any* place or location. There is an almost endless list of criminal offenses, for example, that can be punished even if they happen to take place in the privacy of one's own home or office (forgery, rape, murder, etc., etc.).

Frankly, if gays could assure us that they would shrink back into the shadows of the privacy for which they demand a legal right (and already have in practice), then the existence of sodomy laws would take on less significance. As long as they kept their homosexual behavior off the streets, out of the office, out of the classroom, out of the courtrooms and legislatures of America, then gays could avoid any anti-gay sentiment from the public and answer only to God for their sin.

But, of course, that has no appeal for gays. It would mean not being able to flaunt their gay lifestyle, not being able to make appeals for special legislation, and not being able to insist that the rest of us acknowledge their immoral lifestyle.

To gays it must be said: If it's privacy you want, then *keep it private!* We weren't the ones who insisted that you come out of the closet!

The best way to keep the public out of one's business is to keep from telling the whole world what you do. By their actions, gays show that they don't have a clue what "live and let live" really means. If they don't want people to throw stones at glass houses, then they ought to have the decency to draw the curtains! The public nature of the gay movement is itself the strongest possible evidence that the great "right of privacy" issue has almost nothing to do with *privacy* and virtually everything to do with *the free, open, and unrestricted exercise of immorality*.

Hermeneutical Déjà Vu

It is crucial to remember that the Constitution says nothing about this so-called right of privacy. In the field of law, what we're looking at is the equivalent of Pastor Robinson's "argument from silence." Just as with the Bible, if you listen closely enough to the Constitution's silence, you can hear whatever you want to hear.

In fact, the parallels between Constitutional analysis and biblical hermeneutics couldn't be closer. In Constitutional law, as in biblical hermeneutics, once you move away from the *objectivity* of original understanding (What did the framers of the Constitution intend?) you move inexorably to the *subjectivity* of judicial legislation

(What do individual judges today personally feel is right?).

Given the sameness of the shift in methods of interpretation, is it any wonder that we should discover sameness of results? The Bible teaches that homosexual behavior is a sin; but pro-gay theologians and pastors believe that, given the right circumstances, it can be "the loving thing to do." Likewise, the Constitution gives no protection whatever for homosexual behavior; but liberal academicians and judges believe that, as a matter of privacy, it ought to be given legal protection.

In fact, when you look at the precise terminology being used by pro-gay theologians and liberal lawyer-types, the parallels get downright spooky! For example, where liberal theologians talk about *justice-love* to rationalize removing "responsible" homosexual behavior from the list of sins, David A. J. Richards of New York University Law School tells us in almost exactly the same language that *"the principle of love as a civil liberty"* makes it impermissible to prohibit "private forms of sexual deviance between consenting adults."[1]

Whoever said methods of interpretation don't really matter!

"Privacy": A Euphemism for Moral Relativism

Of course, at this point in legal history it's no good to moan about the fact that the so-called right of privacy is a legal fiction made up out of thin air, *and is therefore itself unconstitutional*. That battle was lost a long time ago. What we must attempt to do for now is to expose "the right of privacy" for what it really is: a euphemism for individual behavior lacking any necessary moral restraint.

Speaking for the dissent in *Hardwick*, Justice Blackmun dredged up the right of privacy (just as he had done in *Roe v. Wade* for abortion) to say, "The fact that individuals define themselves in a significant way through their

intimate sexual relationships with others suggests, in a
nation as diverse as ours, that there may be many 'right'
ways of conducting those relationships. . . ."

If the so-called "right of privacy" means anything, it
means moral relativism. That's because the notion of
privacy dismisses any interest that society might have
and focuses instead on the individual and his or her
personal choice in whatever conduct may be contemplated, whether it is homosexual behavior or, say, abortion.

As Justice Blackmun put it, *Hardwick* was not about a
fundamental right to engage in homosexual sodomy but
about "'the most comprehensive of rights and the right
most valued by civilized men,' namely, 'the right to be let
alone.'"

Of course, there is no Constitutional right "to be let
alone," any more than there is some fill-in-the-blank
"right of privacy." If there were, there could be no law
whatsoever. Can't you just see the accused murderer
saying to the judge, "But Your Honor, the prosecution
can't bring this charge against me. I have a Constitutional right to be let alone!"

What Justice Blackmun really means is that the Constitution, as he interprets it, allows anything which is
consistent with his own (liberal-agenda) notion of morality (and does *not* allow anything—like the prohibition
of sodomy—which does *not* fit his own notion of morality.) But he has already said that in a diverse society there
may be "many right ways," and that means he *must* give
the murderer the same right of privacy to choose his
actions—or else admit that society has the right to tell its
citizens what it disapproves of.

Taken to its logical extreme, moral relativism can
never meet the test of consistency. Its fiercest defenders
are eventually forced to abandon it in their own self-
defense.

But that in a nutshell is what the great cultural war is all about: whether as a society we will give legitimacy to moral relativism or whether we will take a stand for moral absolutes. Homosexual behavior and abortion happen to be the most crucial battlegrounds, but the war is bigger than either of those important issues standing alone. It is a question of socially recognized morality: Does it exist? Can we define it? And, most of all, can we impose it on those who disagree?

As for the last question—"Can we impose our values on others?"—the gay lobby itself has resoundingly answered in the affirmative. Nobody does it better!

Legislating Morality

Ask anyone you meet on the street and they'll tell you, "You can't legislate morality." But of course we *do* legislate morality! Criminal laws in particular are nothing more than the imposition of morality on society. Murder, the "malicious killing of one human being by another, in the absence of justification, excuse, or mitigation" is at its base nothing more than "Thou shalt not kill." Virtually *every* law, whether civil or criminal, can be reduced to some moral judgment.

And what is all the gay-rights activity about if not an attempt to legislate morality? (At least morality as the gays see it.) If *morality* can be legislated, so can *immorality*. Just ask the homosexuals who were put to death under official sanction in Nazi Germany.

If what we mean by "You can't legislate morality" is that you can't always do it *effectively*, then there is some truth to that. "Prohibition," for example, proved to be unenforceable. But that is a question of *practicality*, not of the legitimacy of having such a law.

Morality for its own sake has always been a legitimate basis for public legislation. If that were not true, we would still have segregation—even slavery. The only

real objection anyone can have to either of those practices is a moral objection, plain and simple.

So don't let anyone tell you that society *can't* legislate
morality, nor even that it *shouldn't*. The old saw about not
legislating morality is rhetoric employed only by unprin-
cipled secularists and those who don't wish to have
some particular morality enforced against them.

Does society's right to regulate personal behavior
include immoral actions done in private? Absolutely!
Judge Robert Bork confesses to having been wrongheaded on that question early in his career, and only
brought to his senses by a hypothetical situation put to
him by his colleague Alex Bickel:

> Suppose, he said, that on an offshore island
> there lived a man who raised puppies entirely
> for the pleasure of torturing them to death. The
> rest of us are not required to witness the tor-
> ture, nor can we hear the screams of the ani-
> mals. We just know what is taking place and
> we are appalled. Can it be that we have no
> right, constitutionally or morally, to enact leg-
> islation against such conduct and to enforce it
> against the sadist?[2]

Judge Bork had to admit that Bickel was right: "Moral
outrage *is* a sufficient ground for prohibitory legislation"—even when the conduct is "private."

But What If There's Consent?

Hypothetical turned into reality recently in England
in a case directly involving homosexuals. The House of
Lords upheld assault convictions against five members
of a nationwide homosexual ring who willingly took part
in sadomasochistic acts of genital torture in their homes.
If you dare imagine it, the genital torture involved sand-
paper, fishhooks, and scalpels.

In an odd sort of way, it was a "victimless" offense. No one was compelled to do anything against his wishes. Yet despite the fact that there was consent by adults to acts done in private, about which no one else complained and which resulted in no permanent injury, the law lords nevertheless said that society was "entitled and bound to protect itself against a cult of violence." For the judges, it was strictly a matter of morality: "Pleasure derived from the infliction of pain is an evil thing."[3]

Gays would be among the last to agree that society has any duty to protect individuals even from themselves, but I was intrigued that in an adjacent column to the above article was yet another, with the headline "Theatre Director Died During Bizarre Sex Act." The director had died in his bed during a sadomasochistic homosexual act. A police spokesman said that the director had asphyxiated on his own vomit while tied to the bed by his wrists.[4] Outrageous, for sure, but both *private* and *consensual*.

Does society have no interest in preserving such people of talent among its citizens, even against themselves if necessary? Is the direct imposition of moral values really that different from, for example, helmet laws imposed on motorcyclists to protect them against their own negligence? Court liberals and gay activists may not think so, but we are still our brothers' keepers. Considering the enormous loss of human resources brought on by death through AIDS, who knows what gifted people would still be among us had we, as a society, dared to "impose our morality" on them.

Separation of Church and State?

If you have ever had any serious discussions with pro-gay advocates, you have undoubtedly heard the argument that morality can't be imposed through legislation because it violates the separation between church and state. Anyone who uses this argument automatically proclaims his ignorance of even the most elementary Constitutional law.

The long line of First Amendment "establishment" cases ("Congress shall make no law respecting the establishment of religion") has nothing to do with "legislating morality," but rather with the question of what the government might or might not do *in aid of religion*. (Can the state provide textbooks or school buses for parochial schools? Can public schools allow students "release time" for Bible studies? Do Christian students have the same access to school facilities as, interestingly, a student gay-rights organization?)

Certainly, religion and the church often intersect with law and morality. But that in itself has never been a basis for invalidating legislation.

When Georgia's Attorney General in *Hardwick* cited biblical passages in support of his argument that traditional Judeo-Christian values proscribed sodomy, it brought a swift response from dissenting justices who saw it as a means of invalidating the statute on the basis of *religious intolerance*. (If you want to send liberals into a tizzy, just casually mention, "As the Bible says. . . ." For liberals, it evokes the specter of witch-hunts, Jim Jones, and the Branch Davidian cult in Waco.)

But just because religion *also* happens to condemn conduct which society finds unacceptable does not automatically invalidate legislation having the effect of implementing both concerns. Otherwise we would have to scrap all of criminal law and a large body of tort and contract law which is based directly on the ancient laws of Moses found in the Bible and taught to a greater or lesser extent by both Jewish and Christian religions.

As we have already seen, there are any number of societies other than our own which have found homosexual behavior to be immoral without any appeal whatsoever to religious sources. The avenues of religion and morality may run parallel to each other, but they are not always a two-way street. That is, religion in theory is always moral, but morality is not exclusively in the domain of religion.

On this point, unfortunately, secularists are totally blinded. They will never be convinced that there isn't always and inevitably a connection between the two. And perhaps they can be forgiven for that, because religious people generally have more open concern for morality than those who profess no religion at all. Ironically (and sadly), the fact that a growing number of theologians and pastors are in league with gay activists is proof that religion and morality are *not* always soul mates.

At Stake: Freedom of Religion

Perhaps it is that fear, unfounded though it may be, that is the cause of so much religiophobia among the liberal set—and, worse yet, the explanation for the all-out assault against the Constitutionally-guaranteed free exercise of religion. *The single most disturbing aspect of the battle over gay rights is the deliberate curtailment of the free exercise of religion in America.*

This, at its heart, is what the cultural war is all about. It's not just *Roe v. Wade* and *Bowers v. Hardwick*. It's *right* versus *wrong*. *Morality* versus *immorality*. *Good* versus *evil*. *Civilization* versus *anarchy*.

Unlike abortion, which demands the freedom to do something which doesn't necessarily compel complicity on the part of others, gay rights always requires those who find homosexual behavior to be morally reprehensible to take some action on behalf of gays. At a minimum (as is also true of abortion), it means requiring society to forgo its inherent right to define its collective moral character. As we have seen, society not only has the right but the responsibility to impose a collective sense of morality.

More serious yet, however, is the fact that *giving gay rights* invariably means *taking away religious rights*. Make no mistake about it: "Gay rights" means the elevation of the right to have immoral homosexual relations over the right to act pursuant to one's religious conscience. Inevitably, it prioritizes immorality over morality.

How does that happen? It happens when my mother (or perhaps yours) puts an ad in the paper to rent out her garage apartment. If a couple shows up at her door and discloses that they are gay, my mother could not in good conscience rent to them. But under a typical gay-rights statute or ordinance, she would be in violation of law for refusing to do so.

Or consider the firm of Christian lawyers who wish to hire only practicing Christians on their staff. Under a typical gay-rights statute or ordinance, they would be put in the position of either violating their own consciences by *hiring*, or violating the law for *refusing to hire* a legal secretary who was openly homosexual.

The lip service paid to "free exercise" when religious organizations are (sometimes) given an exception to gay-rights statutes is wholly inadequate. "Free exercise" was not intended primarily for religious *organizations*, but for religious *individuals*.

Pro-gay legislators, city councillors, and judges naively assume that they need to protect gays against some hateful desire to discriminate against homosexuals. What they fail to appreciate (or are too morally blind to see) is that it is not *hatred* from which we operate but *conscience*. It is not the *homosexual* we can't live with if we cave in to our beliefs, but *ourselves*.

In the give-and-take of individual rights, which by necessity share the same space and time, there is no room for compromise—only competition. Once you square off relative morality against absolute morality, it is a fight to the death. They can't both survive.

One would assume that when any piece of gay-rights legislation is proposed, attention would be paid to the tandem concerns of gay rights and free exercise of religion. Surely, we think, someone is asking what happens when they come into conflict.

Unfortunately, "sexual orientation" (gay rights) tends to be treated as any other garden-variety "right," like race, gender, and physical handicap—none of which have any moral implications for those who might be called upon to respond to their plea for nondiscrimination. With "sexual orientation," legislatures and courts not only fail to consider the impact of gay rights on free exercise, but seemingly don't care!

Consider the dissenting opinion in the California case which upheld the right of a Catholic couple to refuse the lease of their apartment to an unmarried couple. Judge Margaret Grignon had little sympathy for Mr. and Mrs. Donahue's rights of religious belief: "The burden on religious conduct from the fair housing law is slight, in that it does not prohibit the Donahues from practicing their religion. The statute does not require the Donahues to aid and abet 'sinners,' it merely requires them to act in a non-discriminatory manner toward all prospective tenants."[5] Obviously, Judge Grignon doesn't have a clue as to what religious conscience is all about.

With that kind of an attitude, worse times are yet to come. What ought to keep you awake tonight is the all-too-real possibility that a book such as this one, or a sermon decrying the sin of sodomy, will one day be punishable under law as a "hate crime." (For now, the Supreme Court has held at least one hate crime statute to be unconstitutional, since it violated the right to free speech. But the case signaled the direction in which gay activists are headed, and you just know that they won't stop until sodomy is legal and our labeling it as sin is a crime.)

Is that merely hysterical scaremongering? Just listen to this: In Britain, under the Labour Campaign for Gay and Lesbian Rights, a proposed offense of incitement to hatred on the grounds of sexual orientation would mean that churches would be forbidden—get this, *forbidden*—to preach that homosexuality is contrary to the Bible![6] It may yet be some time before the charter's intent is given official sanction, but one should never doubt but that this is the ultimate aim of a godless gay-rights movement.

Of this you can be sure: To whatever extent gay rights are given free rein in governmental edicts, freedom of religion is sure to be restricted.

Free Exercise Is No Longer Compelling

The court cases addressing the free exercise of religion when it intersects with gay-rights legislation have proved to be a mixed bag. In 1980 a California court in *Walker v. First Presbyterian Church* held that, despite a gay-rights ordinance, the constitution exempted the church from having to hire a gay organist.[7]

But on the opposite coast in 1987, an almost-incredible application was made of the Washington D.C. Human Rights ordinance set out in the previous chapter. In *Gay Rights Coalition v. Georgetown University*,[8] the court agreed that the Catholic-affiliated university did not have to "recognize" a student gay-rights group, but it did have to "permit access" to university facilities just as with all other student organizations.

On the point of giving gays equal access, the D.C. opinion recognized Georgetown's free-exercise interest in excluding gay organizations, but said that such interest was overcome by the District of Columbia's "compelling interest" in nondiscrimination. (You may recall that "compelling interest" had been rejected by the Supreme Court in *Hardwick* only a year earlier, and that in any event this test should apply only to government discrimination, not the act of a private institution.)

What Christians need to understand is that the D.C. court's ruling applied the very highest level of scrutiny ("compelling interest") to alleged rights for homosexuals, which are never once hinted at in the Constitution, while relegating to the very lowest level of scrutiny the specifically-enumerated right of free exercise. Wake up, America! Christian belief is at risk!

Of course, the Georgetown case was decided at a local level (where more and more similar cases are sneaking up on us without getting national publicity). Fortunately, Congress has somewhat atoned for the sin by enacting legislation which now exempts religiously affiliated institutions like Georgetown from the odious "sexual orientation" provision of the D.C. ordinance.

But the wider impact on free exercise was yet to come, in the 1990 case of *Employment Div., Dep't of Human Resources v. Smith*.[9] I can't begin to tell you how potentially devastating this case is for Christians. Quite amazingly, Justice Scalia (one of our few "conservative" justices!) rejected the compelling state-interest test in free-exercise cases where government action has only some "incidental" effect on religious conscience. What that means is that the exercise of religion is no longer regarded as a "fundamental right" worthy of the protection given to all other fundamental rights.

Where does that leave free exercise of religion when it conflicts with gay-rights laws? Justice Scalia gave us only the slightest hint in a footnote. It may leave us in a *balancing* act, where the court can decide that *on balance* gay rights outweigh free exercise. (Using whose scales?)

Or it may leave us facing the so-called "rational basis" test, which would allow gays to override free exercise of religion as long as the government could show virtually any "rational basis" for gay-rights legislation. It takes hardly any showing to meet that fragile test—perhaps only the need in California, let's say, to bolster the state's entertainment industry, in which there has been a historical connection with homosexuals. Who knows? It wouldn't take much.

Fortunately, under their own constitutions, several states have already ignored the new federal rule and provided greater free-exercise protection. (The *Donahue* case mentioned above is one such laudable result.) But you can see how far we have come from the intent of the framers of the Constitution, many of whom came to this country for the express purpose of achieving religious liberty. They had to fight a revolutionary war to secure such liberty. Today we are in the midst of our own cultural war to maintain that very freedom. In this war, the enemy is not wearing red coats, but red ribbons.

The Hypocrisy of Pluralism

If you listen closely to the gay-rights debate, you hear a lot of talk about pluralism—the need to recognize diversity within the community, including women, blacks, and, of course, homosexuals. But in fact, what this really means is virtually any group and every group except Christians. When it comes to pluralism, Christians don't count.

Commenting on the outrageous Georgetown case, columnist George Will said it was "an assault on pluralism, waged with the rhetoric of pluralism. It is an example of how the proliferation of 'rights' threatens freedom."[10] And with that we're back to where we started: One person's rights always threaten another's freedom. But gays don't care whose rights they threaten in pursuing their own right to publicly flaunt their lifestyle. In fact, one gets the distinct impression that gays deliberately and premeditatedly want to *force* people of faith to give up their right of conscience. *They* already have; why shouldn't everybody else!

That attitude was recently made clear to our law faculty at Pepperdine University. As a Christian law school, we were dismayed to hear from one of our accrediting bodies, the American Association of Law Schools (AALS), that the "sexual orientation" provisions in its bylaws was to be enforced even against member schools having a religious affiliation.

It was not enough that there are very few such law schools in the nation, nor that few gay activists would likely choose to attend a school with such a religious profile in the first place. Rather than promoting the pluralism which receives almost worshipful reverence when applied to the liberal agenda, pluralism was now being trashed in the name of gay rights.

In fact, in the name of "pluralism" and "diversity," member schools were being required to engage in affirmative action programs, even to the point of requiring any potential *employers* of the school's graduates to follow the same nondiscriminatory guidelines! (Did someone say something about a "right of privacy?")

Beyond the Reach of the Law

What is important about this illustration is that we are no longer talking merely about *government* influence through the courts or legislatures; AALS is a *private* organization. And it just happens to be a private organization that, because of its accrediting power, is crucial for any law school desiring recognition for its scholastic excellence.

You should also know that many major corporations have already adopted personnel policies that are non-discriminatory with reference to "sexual orientation." These include ABC, American Motors, Anheuser-Busch, Apple Computers, Avon, Bank of America, Ben and Jerry's, General Electric, Honeywell, Microsoft, Shearson American Express, Silicon Graphics, Standard Oil of California, and TRW Corp, to name just a few.[11] (Enough, in fact, to refute 1) the argument that gays are "politically powerless," and 2) that they are in need of special judicial protection.)

Perhaps you've heard all the uproar over the Boy Scouts' refusal to have gays as either members or leaders. They can't seem to win either way they turn. On one hand, the Scouts have been sued because a scoutmaster who turned out to be a homosexual had sexually molested two young scouts. On the other hand, their funding has been cut off by San Francisco's United Way chapter (to be expected) and by Levi Strauss (not to be expected), the makers of Levi's and Dockers clothing.

Whether it be in government, business, or voluntary associations, the commitment and dedication of the gay movement seems to have no limits. There is simply no stone left unturned when gay activists go to work.

We *Must* Discriminate!

It is tempting for Christians to say, "We don't mean to discriminate against anyone; we simply don't want to give gays any special rights." That sounds palatable, because no one wants to be guilty of discrimination. The very word *discrimination* seems somehow unchristian. But not wanting to give gays special rights *is* a form of discrimination. And there is no reason to apologize for it. We have every right to discriminate, and even the responsibility of doing so.

Every time we exercise discretion in housing and hiring decisions, we are discriminating. When we choose applicant "A" for the manager's position and not applicant "B", we have just discriminated. (It doesn't have to be discrimination *against* applicant "B". It could simply be discrimination *in favor of* applicant "A".)

More importantly, that discrimination may well have been on the basis of character—*moral* character. That's why we have applicants provide letters of recommendation, and why application forms request recommenders to comment on the applicant's moral character. (I'll never forget the recommendation letter we received on behalf of a student applying for admission to the law school. The writer was obviously confused in his terminology, as evidenced by his statement—meant to be favorable—that "this young man is of the very highest moral turpitude"!)

Improper discrimination makes housing and hiring decisions on the basis of irrelevant factors such as race and gender. Character, by contrast is rarely irrelevant. Just ask political candidates and officeholders whose "private" lives have come to public attention. The irony is that there are any number of pro-gay supporters out there who think Senator Robert Packwood ought to forfeit his office because of *heterosexual* impropriety, but who think nothing of asking society to officially accept *homosexual* impropriety. The pro-gay camp's "sound moral judgment" is the religious right's "discrimination."

Properly used, discrimination in matters of morals is indeed "sound moral judgment." And who can be faulted for exercising it? As Christians we have no option. In a nation daily facing the ravages of moral slippage, we have an increased responsibility to discriminate between right and wrong, good and evil.

Let no one think that the struggle over gay rights is merely a political issue, like the budget deficit or health care. Far from it, the struggle over gay rights is nothing short of an all-out cultural war in which gay activists are the shock troops for the Enemy. It's not just gay rights that are at stake for those who wish to act immorally. For the rest of us, what is at risk in this cultural war is nothing less than the right to follow our consciences and to freely and boldly exercise our faith.

Will we Christians be any match for militant gays? All we have to do in order to lose is to believe that "free exercise" is strictly a "private matter." Never has the cliché "use it or lose it" been more apropos. *Now* is the time for Christians to act. If we sit back and let the gays have their way with us, there will be no one around to care when we finally cry out in desperation that our religious rights have been sodomized!

CHAPTER 13

Dismantling the Nuclear Family

The family unit—spawning ground of lies, be-trayals, mediocrity, hypocrisy and violence—will be abolished. The family unit, which only dampens imagination and curbs free will, must be eliminated.
—Michael Swift, "For the
Homoerotic Order," in
Gay Community News

Have you seen the billboards showing the lesbian couple, one quite obviously pregnant? The message to the side says: Another traditional family.

The billboards (with various other scenes depicting gay and lesbian couples) are sponsored by GLAAD, the Gay and Lesbian Alliance Against Defamation. A spokes-person for the break-the-family-stereotype billboards says, "We hope this is the beginning of a series showing many different kinds of gay and lesbian families."

You're not likely to have seen the Australian advertise-ment done by Toyota, which was intended for the gay market. In the ad, the heading reads "The family car." Beneath it is a picture showing a sedate Toyota hatch-back, along with a gay couple—supposedly a "family" like any other, complete with their two . . . dogs.

Thanks to the gay-rights movement, the traditional family today is under attack like never before. The word *traditional* had to be added when the word *family* became the subject of redefinition. Now it seems that even *traditional family* is being hijacked. Today, a "traditional family" is whatever the participants choose to define as a family.

But aren't you curious about those billboards? If gay and lesbian couples are really that "traditional," then why do they have to spend thousands of dollars on billboard advertising to *convince* us! If something is "traditional," isn't it by definition something that everyone recognizes as part of a long-standing heritage? What kind of long-standing heritage are we talking about with gay and lesbian "families"? Five years? Ten years? Three decades? (That's barely one generation.)

And what about that expectant lesbian mother? Is her pregnancy a *traditional pregnancy*? Or can we infer anything from the fact that insemination for lesbians almost always comes accompanied with the word *artificial*? (Sure, heterosexuals sometimes have to resort to artificial insemination when natural methods fail, but at least the donor father is usually around after the conception to call the child his own. Traditionally speaking, that is.)

What Is a Family?

Did you ever think you would see the day when anybody had to ask what a family was? But now that question is all the rage. In fact, for the first time the 1990 Census included a question aimed at identifying unmarried couples who live together, both heterosexual and homosexual.

The so-called "nuclear family," of course, has always been husband and wife, parent and child. The "extended family" would include grandparents, aunts and uncles, nieces and nephews, cousins, and to the delight of everyone as time goes on, grandchildren!

But the times are changing. In California, the state Joint Select Task Force on the Changing Family issued a report in 1989 in which they judiciously refused to define "family." Instead, they chose to define the *functions* of a family: "To care for the emotional and physical needs of its own; provide them with love and security; shape their values and social skills, and provide a haven from outside stresses."[1] Naturally, that allows room for lesbian and gay "families" who supposedly can perform all those functions. (More later, but that bit about "shaping their values" alone ought to raise red flags!)

Of course, that definition also might include groups of unrelated singles who live separately but "function as a family, sharing holidays, triumphs and tragedies," as reporter Beverly Beyette put it.[2] Or, as she suggests, what about "commune-type families who choose to live an ecologically gentle way of life in nonsmoking, vegetarian homes, sharing rent and chores?"

Once family is defined as *function*, the possible permutations boggle the mind. How about a 45-year-old homosexual and his 14-year-old "companion"? (The North American Man-Boy Love Association has that seriously on its agenda.) Or how about Woody Allen and his 22-year-old adopted stepdaughter Soon-Ye Previn? They've already had a loving sexual relationship, and of course the traditional "family" photos of Soon-Ye nude on the couch.

The whole Woody Allen-Mia Farrow fiasco is nothing if not the perfect illustration of what happens when we toss the traditional family aside! They may have *functioned* as a family—adopted children and all—but the essence of a marriage commitment between a man and a woman was obviously lacking. And a stepdaughter who should have been able to trust Allen for the function of "love and security" ended up only a technicality away from being the victim of incest. (Of course, I know—incest happens in traditional families as well. But at least when it happens in traditional families we have a clearly defined object of outrage. With Woody we weren't quite sure.)

The ploy that is used in the process of redefinition is to destroy the notion of a "nuclear family." After all, everybody knows that fewer and fewer households today include mom, dad, and the kids. It's considered only a matter of demographics: "families" ought to be whatever "families" are. And owing to widespread divorce, single-parent households, and unmarried living arrangements, families aren't what they used to be.

By its nature, seduction is always subtle. But this seductive ploy deserves a prize. Who can deny that "not every family has mom, dad, and kids"? My father, for example, grew up in a family with four brothers and a mother. His father died when Dad was only five, and yet Dad managed to grow up as a fine, decent human being.

Like Dad, millions of people have been raised in circumstances where one or another component of the nuclear family was missing. And they were no less a "traditional family."

So what is the only logical conclusion? To be a family, you don't necessarily have to have a "mom" or a "dad" or "kids," and therefore (and therefore?) the family can be *any combination of the above*: *two* "moms," *two* "dads"— whatever suits your fancy.

I say again, the logic simply boggles the mind!

Some Damning Admissions

It's worth taking a close look at what gays themselves are saying about the kind of "families" they would have us approve. Take, for example, Brian Mossop, who has mounted a challenge to the Canadian Supreme Court to have his homosexual relationship given family status. His lover, Ken Popert, says, "I am in a web of relationships, but there is no centre and no boundaries. It's not structured and institutionalized, the way the family is.

Each person can feel at the centre of it—because it has no centre."[3]

Popert is telling it straight: The gay "family" is nothing like the traditional family, with its center and boundaries, its structure and institution. An amorphous fluidity may work for amoebae, but not for families. Families *need* structure and roles and clearly defined boundaries.

In their book *The Male Couple: How Relationships Develop*,[4] Dr. David McWhirter and Dr. Andrew Mattison (homosexual lecturers at the University of California at San Diego's School of Medicine) tell us that gay couples "assume an equality in the relationship which is not present in most heterosexual marriages."

All right, so there's more equality with gay couples. What about being the "traditional family"?

"It is not true," they say, "that in most lasting gay relationships one male assumes the sexual, emotional and practical role of 'the husband' and the other the stereotyped role of 'the wife.'"

So what are you telling us? Aren't you confirming what we already knew—that gays don't have "traditional families" after all?

"What counts most in any relationship, homo- or heterosexual, are the building blocks of shared experiences which lead to trust and tolerance and love."

That makes sense. How is it working with gay couples?

"Gay men," says McWhirter, "lose their passion, infatuation and romance—what we call 'limerence'—within one year in many cases. I don't know why. Probably because there are no children to hold the relationship together, or they never believed in the first place that it would last."[5]

You mean, gay "families" don't work well because they aren't "traditional families"? Yes. I think we understand what you're saying.

"Domestic Partners"—Sort of Married

As of yet, no state in the union recognizes marriages between gays. So far, even the law appreciates that "gay marriage" is an oxymoron. But at least 19 cities across America now recognize what they call "domestic partners," who may register as couples and receive a variety of legal benefits as a result. The pro-gay cities include San Francisco, Los Angeles, Berkeley, and Santa Cruz in California; Minneapolis, Minnesota; Madison, Wisconsin; Tacoma Park, Maryland; and Cambridge, Massachusetts.

San Francisco's domestic-partner ordinance (which includes heterosexual couples) was voted in at the end of 1990 and has remained intact despite attempts at repeal. In a twist to "traditional Christian marriage," in order for couples to register under the ordinance, they *must already have lived together* for six months prior to applying for the certificate!

Ironically, the first opportunity for gay couples to register was Valentine's Day, 1991. (They just *loved* the symbolism!) Lesbians Ruth Mahaney and Nina Jo Smith were cheered when they descended the City Hall steps with the first domestic-partners certificate in hand. Within a year, a thousand couples had registered, and 13 of the couples had filed for dissolution, including Jean Harris, one of Mayor Jordan's gay assistants who had pushed for the ordinance.[6]

The ordinance itself was all a grand deception on the part of gay activists. A previously proposed ordinance which had included social and economic benefits for domestic partners was struck down by the voters. To boost the chances of success for the later ordinance proposal, the benefits package was cut out, and backers said, "There is nothing hidden, no unanticipated costs, no bill to come due for tomorrow's taxpayers." Of course, it was an out-and-out lie.

Despite personal promises from gay supervisor Harry Britt that the domestic partner ordinance which he authored would not confer any financial benefits, within seven weeks he had cast the deciding vote to give city-funded benefits to city employees who had filed for domestic partner certificates. The Mayor's Task Force on Family Policy estimated that the benefits would cost San Francisco taxpayers a *million-plus dollars annually*.[7] At least the costs are no longer hidden!

Britt is now pushing for domestic-partners recognition in private business. That's the way the gays work. They nibble away, little by little, using deception if necessary. Today it's just a slight change in the law. Tomorrow it's just another slight change, and the next day yet another. Before we know it, we are footing the bill for their immoral liaisons.

The Push for Gay Marriages

It is openly acknowledged that the whole concept of "domestic partners" is but a stepping-stone to full recognition of gay marriages, with all its rights and privileges (if not traditional responsibilities). That was the point being made in the April 1992 "wed-in" in Washington D.C., in which the Rev. Troy Perry performed a mass "ceremony of union" for a 1000 gay couples.

On the legal scene, the most shocking development of late comes to us from Hawaii where, in the case of *Baehr v. Lewin*, the Supreme Court of Hawaii declared that the statute regulating marriage licenses is vulnerable to challenge under the equal protection clause of the state's Constitution. What that translates into is the strong possibility that a rehearing of the case will result in the legalization of gay marriages in the state of Hawaii.

Two aspects of the case are particularly noteworthy. First, the Court specifically rejected the contention that gays have a fundamental right to same-sex marriages arising out of the right to privacy or otherwise. The Court said it "must look not to 'personal private notions,' but to the 'traditions and [collective] conscience of our people' to determine whether a principle is 'so rooted [there] . . . as to be ranked as fundamental." The Court acknowledges society's right to impose its *collective conscience*, if not its *morality*, to reject same-sex marriages.

But what the Court gives, the Court then takes away. Torturing logic to the extreme, the Court poses the possibility that same-sex marriages need not involve either gays or lesbians. Under the Hawaii statute, even two perfectly *heterosexual* partners of the same gender would be prohibited from marrying, and thereby miss out on the package of economic and other benefits to which married couples are entitled. Therefore (in deference to the multitude of heterosexuals who undoubtedly are clamoring to marry persons of their own gender!), such sex discrimination denies equal protection to same-gender couples.

By that logic, of course, any person of either gender who chooses to remain *single* is also deprived of the marital benefits package and thus is also denied equal protection! Did it never occur to the Court that most family benefits are intended to promote, not just marriages, but marriages which typically result in *families*? Homosexuals and single heterosexuals don't exactly fit the need being addressed.

The most disturbing aspect of the Hawaii case is the Court's redefinition of marriage as nothing more than an economic unit: "a partnership to which both partners bring their financial resources as well as their individual energies and efforts." Did the Court so quickly forget that society's "collective conscience" has viewed marriage as a bond of relational commitment far beyond mere contract? (Why else the official recognition of ceremonies performed in a religious context by ministers speaking of sacred vows and "what God has joined together"?)

Naturally, the Court rushed to defend sections of the statute that prohibited marriages involving infancy, incest, or bigamy (moral judgments all), seeming oblivious to the hypocrisy of opening the way for homosexual marriages despite the lip service paid to society's collective conscience.

Bigamy, in particular, tells the tale. Replace *bigamy* with *polygamy* (which it is), and you have the case of *Reynolds v. United States* to deal with. In 1878, the U.S. Supreme Court extolled the virtues of the "wall of separation" between church and state, and then proceeded to tell Mormons that they could not practice polygamy, despite their religious beliefs. Why? Because "polygamy has always been odious among the northern and western nations of Europe . . ." and because "it is impossible to believe that the constitution . . . was intended to prohibit legislation in respect to this most important feature of social life."

What irony! Mormons, acting pursuant to constitutionally protected freedom of religion, may not practice heterosexual polygamy (of but questionable morality, given its practice in biblical times); but gays, having no constitutional protection whatever, may practice (patently immoral) homosexual marriage! So much for the ACLU's inevitable cries of "Separation between church and state!" and "You can't legislate morality!" Whether it be polygamy, bigamy, incest, or homosexual marriage—the state has every right to restrict marital unions solely on the basis of moral considerations.

If it's a matter of equal protection in a moral vacuum, then equal protection demands that the state recognize marriages between a homosexual father and his son; between a forty-year-old gay and his nine-year-old love object; and between, not just two, but three gay lovers.

The Hawaii Supreme Court justifies its decision by analogy to the landmark *Loving v. Virginia* case in which the U.S. Supreme Court struck down miscegenation laws prohibiting marriages between persons of different race. The Hawaii Court took great delight in pointing out that miscegenation laws had been justified by religious folks asserting that in God's eyes an interracial marriage was "not a marriage." If religious folks were wrong about interracial marriages, then surely religious folks today are equally wrongheaded to say that homosexual marriage is "not a marriage."

What can I say? Sometimes religious folks *are* dead wrong. (A lot of Christians once theologically contended that the earth was flat.) Yet had you asked Moses about miscegenation laws, he too would have soundly rejected them. He himself had an interracial marriage (and experienced taunting discrimination by his own siblings). But it was the same Moses who conveyed God's law: "Do not lie with a man as with a woman." While race is only tangentially related to the essence of marriage (as in the *color* of the man and the woman), gender is its very soul! Marriage is nothing if not the celebration of gender differences joined in a complementary union.

My first reaction to the Hawaii decision is to wonder if it's not all a public relations ploy to have every gay couple in America flying to Honolulu to get married and to stay for the honeymoon, thereby boosting the Hawaiian economy. But it's not just about swaying palms and gay marriages in the fiftieth state. There is an enormous legal problem about to drop like a coconut. It's known as the "full faith and credit" clause. If *Hawaii* proceeds to legalize gay marriages, homosexuals will certainly demand that *all other states* recognize the Hawaii marriage, just as is the case with heterosexual marriages.

And what vestige of control will the military then have over a gay soldier who goes off to Hawaii on furlough to marry his bunkmate? Benefits for military spouses are likely to be in complete turmoil; military housing will be revolutionized; and the compromise ban on gays in the military will have been all but lifted.

And why all of this? Because a handful of social-planning jurists in a single state have radically redefined a centuries-old consensus about what constitutes the most fundamental relationship known to humankind. "And the two shall become one flesh" has never been so debased.

Why Bother?

If you are wondering why gays even bother to bring up the subject of marriage, there are three significant reasons. The first reason is genuine enough. Just because they are gay doesn't mean that they have no mating instincts. Virtually everyone longs for love and companionship.

Even so, I suspect that for many gays there is a second reason: that having something like marital status is important in helping them come to grips with their own abnormal lifestyle. Deep down, not many people really want to be considered odd or out of step with everybody else. It's also a way to deal with the guilt. Even when one is out of the closet, there is still the mighty struggle to convince one's self that homosexual behavior is right. Marriage for gays would be another comforting closet.

Of more practical importance is the third reason: *spin-off legal benefits that only accompany marriage.* As is so wonderfully illustrated in the San Francisco experience, it's not all love and kisses. It's mostly a matter of finance, and implications relating to the division of property, employee benefits, and insurance coverage. Listen to the following news briefs:

In Denver, civil liberties lawyers hailed an administrative ruling that a lesbian "spouse" is entitled to sick-leave pay reserved for immediate family members of city workers. Mary Ross had claimed three days of (compensated) leave to care for her "permanent life partner" during an illness and follow-up tests.[8]

In New York, a suit filed by the Gay Teachers Association (Is *that* a sickening thought!) claims that the teachers have been unfairly denied medical-insurance coverage for their long-term partners, a benefit available to spouses in "traditional families."[9]

In California, Boyce Hinman asked that his homosexual partner of 12 years be covered as a "spouse" under the State Employees' Dental Care Act. Even his union filed an *amicus* (friend of the court) brief in support of his claim.[10]

Larry Brinkin, who was denied a (compensated) funeral leave when his gay partner of 11 years died, said that his right to privacy was violated, and that the discrimination was in violation of the California Fair Employment Act.[11]

Allen Chamberlain challenged his employer's policy of providing reduced air travel benefits to family members of heterosexual employees but denying the same deal to Chamberlain and his lover of nine years.[12]

Summing it all up, Leonard Graff, legal director of National Gay Rights Advocates in San Francisco, said that the easiest way to end much employment discrimination against gays is to allow homosexual marriage.[13] Never doubt that there is always method to the gay madness!

Are Benefits Such a Big Deal?

I have to admit, I can't get very excited one way or the other about discrimination when it comes to employee travel benefits. Who cares whether only married employees reap the benefit of group purchasing power? But I doubt if the "marriage" policy in such cases was part of any sinister plot to exclude either gay or heterosexual singles or couples. Rather than being evidence of homophobia or even heterosexual live-in-ophobia, more likely it was simply a benefit extended to traditional families in recognition of the greater economic impact on married couples, particularly where there are children.

Where it starts to get more interesting is in employment policies related to compensated sick leave and funeral leave. Again, if you replay the history of such policies, you find that they invariably arose during times when the traditional family—*being traditional*—was simply *assumed*. There was nothing conspiratorial about it.

When alternative lifestyles began cropping up, there was still no reason to change. Heterosexuals who began openly living together without benefit of marriage weren't raising a stink. With but rare exceptions, they realized that it was *they* who were out of step with everyone else, and that any disparity of treatment was just the price they paid for it. If they wanted the benefits badly enough, they could always formalize their relationships through marriage and that would do it.

Of course, that's exactly the point being pressed by gays. As homosexuals, they aren't *permitted* to formalize their relationships through marriage so as to reap the benefits. But is that because society is bent on penalizing homosexuals?

Gays may consider this is a distinction without a difference, but the difference is legitimate: Rather than being intended as a *penalty* to homosexuals, family benefits have always been meant as an *incentive* for the glue that holds society together: the family. Family benefits provided by both government and private industry have always been part of a conscious social policy for the encouragement, support, and affirmation of the traditional family. Why? Because the traditional family represents and fosters social stability, strength, and continuity.

Lets face it—marriage-and-family is a difficult enterprise, deserving of all the external support it can get.

Every penny spent in the direction of families is a long-term investment in the nation's future.

This is not to say that unmarried individuals contribute any less to society. (The proverbial "old maid schoolteacher" may have had more impact for good than any number of married teachers with families.) Before my own marriage, I never felt that I was not a contributing member of society. Nor did I ever once resent any benefits offered to married people to which I was not entitled. Like most singles, I understood and applauded the good sense of family-oriented policies.

So why do gays push for special legislation in their favor when it comes to employment benefits? (Remember that for the most part any "family policy discrimination" applies to heterosexual singles and couples as well as to gays.) The only answer can be *to press for the legitimacy of their lifestyle—fully subsidized by the rest of society.*

"Not only do we want to live in sin," gays are telling us, "but we want *you* to pay for it!"

Are Gay Rights Special Rights?

The mere mention of "special rights" will draw fire from gay activists every time. As one pro-gay editorial protested: "Civil rights guarantees are not, as some claim, 'special rights.' They are affirmations of equal rights." But that line simply begs the question: Is homosexual behavior either a "civil right" or "equally protected" by the Constitution? The Supreme Court has already said "No!"

As indicated above, family policy benefits are themselves a form of *special* rights. And it is those same special rights that gay activists covet. So why the innocent pretense to the contrary?

When compared to heterosexual couples similarly disaffected by family policy benefits, why should gay couples have any greater rights? Being well aware of the force of this argument, gays usually include unmarried heterosexual couples in their domestic partner packages. They need all the allies they can get.

Just to show, however, that gays sometimes demand special rights even beyond their heterosexual brothers and sisters who live in sin outside of marriage, note the recent action by BART, the (San Francisco-Oakland) Bay Area Rapid Transit. BART directors have approved giving health benefits to partners of gay and lesbian employees, but have specifically *excluded* unmarried heterosexual couples from the employment package![14] If that's not "special rights" for gays, what is it?

And, of course, when it comes to housing and employment, gays want special rights, not only beyond those given to heterosexual couples (who, as seen earlier in the *Donahue* case, are provided no similar protection in renting an apartment), but also special exemption from having their moral character scrutinized (something that none of us heterosexuals can legally avoid, whether married or single).

The Gay Adoption Frenzy

In one particular area of the movement for gay rights, we find a crossover between the push for special rights and the overall challenge to the traditional family. It's the matter of gay adoptions. (Similar concerns are often involved in child-custody disputes where one of two natural parents surfaces as a homosexual.) The question which always arises is, Should adoption (or custody) be adversely affected because of one's homosexual status?

The courts have taken three basic approaches in answering that question. Many courts find homosexuals unfit parents per se. Others require proof of some connection between the parent's homosexual conduct and any alleged harm which might befall the child. Still others consider homosexual status to be simply one of many factors to be considered in assessing what might be in the best interest of the child.

It is important to note that there is no fundamental right involved in adoption cases. The privilege to adopt is a "permissive right" which is regulated by the state. Although the state cannot act capriciously, it may deny adoption on almost any reasonable basis. Moral concerns alone would be enough.

What then are the factors that may be considered as a basis for denying homosexuals the privilege to adopt? The two suggested factors carrying perhaps the least weight are 1) the fear of molestation, and 2) fear of contracting AIDS. There is little evidence to support the "molestation factor." And evidence of AIDS transmission is absolutely nil (the reasons for which we shall see in the next chapter).

Of more concern to the courts is 3) the potential for the child being stigmatized, embarrassed, and possibly bullied by other children. Anecdotal evidence of bullying runs both ways. Expert witnesses are available to support everything from "it never happens" to "bullying is common to children in these circumstances." However, even gays, through such books as *Heather Has Two Mommies*, acknowledge that the problem of stigmatization is real. Their only defense is to blame a homophobic society, as if young children themselves don't intuitively know that something is wrong with Heather having two mommies! "Out of the mouths of babes" says it all.

Then there is 4) the concern that the child will become a homosexual by imitating his or her gay parents. The gays have a favorite response to this concern: "We all had heterosexual parents and we've grown up lesbian and gay." Gays usually add another follow-up sentence, but, interestingly, not the same sentence. Some say, "You can't change whatever orientation you were born with." Others forget what's at stake and give away the game.

In a recent BBC television program entitled "Fostering Prejudice," a lesbian made the more honest admission: "People make their own choices about their sexuality. I think that a good parent offers different choices about sexuality and I certainly wouldn't be saying that our way is necessarily right for our children."[15]

If she is right about the homosexual lifestyle being a matter of choice (and of course she is), then having gay parents must surely have *some* impact on that decision-making process in a young child. At a minimum, it tells the child that the homosexual lifestyle is a morally legitimate option, which it is not.

Finally, there is 5) the concern that a child would be exposed to an immoral environment. This reason alone ought to be sufficient cause to deny the right of adoptive parenthood to homosexuals. Are we to believe that the child will grow up unaware of homosexual behavior in even its most benign forms? There is simply no way that children should be exposed daily to conduct which for some 35 centuries has been almost universally recognized as morally reprehensible.

But Christians, of all people, need to realize that there is an Achilles' heel to even this compelling argument. Placement agencies are quite aware of the sound reasons against homosexual parenting, and they usually act accordingly. Nevertheless, they are understandably concerned about the so-called "unadoptable" children—those children who are physically handicapped, or from racial minorities, or who manifest severe behavior problems. More and more gay couples are saying, "If no one else is willing, we will take the outcasts. After all, we too are outcasts."

And what will our answer be to that? The last thing outcast children need is outcast parents, and having homosexual parents will only add to their problems. But *what will our answer be to that?* As Christians, it is time that we put our money—and our love and our commitment —where our mouth is.

Educating the Next Generation

Gays are beginning at the most elementary levels to cultivate the idea of gay families in the minds of a new generation. And I literally mean "elementary," as in elementary schools. Only an alert school board prevented former Chancellor Joseph Fernandez from instituting the so-called "children of the rainbow curriculum" in District 24 in New York City's Borough of Queens.

The purpose of the curriculum was to indoctrinate children with particular attitudes about, among other things, homosexual conduct. If the chancellor had been given his way (he is now on his way out), impressionable young students would have been exposed to books such as those published by Alyson Wonderland, the imprint for Alyson Publications of Boston.[16]

I picked up a copy of one of their books, *Daddy's Roommate*, by Michael Willhoite, at a general bookstore in Fort Worth, Texas. It was right there on the shelf next to the real *Alice in Wonderland*. Alice would never believe the "wonderland" we are thrusting upon young people today. *Daddy's Roommate* is illustrated for children ages three to eight, and has a simple story line:

> My Mommy and Daddy got a divorce last year.
> Now there's somebody new at Daddy's house.
> Daddy and his roommate Frank live together,
> Work together,
> Eat together,
> Sleep together,
> Shave together,
> And sometimes even fight together.
> But they always make up. . . .
> Mother says Daddy and Frank are gay.

At first I didn't know what that meant.
So she explained it.
Being gay is just one more kind of love.
And love is the best kind of happiness.
Daddy and his roommate are very happy together,
And I'm happy too![17]

Now there's a great bedtime story for three-year-olds: A happy picture of just another traditional family!

Other books in the series include, *Heather Has Two Mommies*: "As the daughter of a lesbian couple, three-year-old Heather sees nothing unusual in having two mommies. When she joins a playgroup and discovers that other children have 'daddies' her confusion is dispelled by an adult instructor and the other children who describe their own different families."[18]

Gloria Goes to Gay Pride tells how little Gloria has a fun day out with her two "mommies" at the gay pride celebrations. A coloring book for children ages two to six, called simply *Families*, depicts a diversity of races, generations, and cultural backgrounds—as well as, of course, gay and lesbians "parents."[19]

How Would You Feel If Your Dad Was Gay? is written for the somewhat older child (ages six to twelve). "When Jasmine announces in class that her dad is gay, her brother complains that she had no right to reveal a fact that he wanted to keep secret. Through Jasmine's experiences and those of Noah, a boy with a lesbian mother, the authors address *many issues facing such children* [my emphasis]."[20]

This last book raises some compelling questions. *What about* the "many issues facing such children"? Even gays have to admit that there are real concerns when we move from heterosexual to homosexual couples. And why are they "issues" at all? If these children were from traditional family homes, there wouldn't be any troubling issues of this nature to face. Goodness knows, kids already face enough crucial issues without burdening them with having two "mommies" or two "daddies."

Give America a generation of this kind of indoctrination, and gay marriages will be all the vogue. Give America a generation of gay marriages, and you'll see a bunch of kids-turned-adults messed up beyond all recognition.

Of Genuine and Counterfeits

The story is told of an exasperated President Lincoln interjecting in the middle of a quibbling Cabinet discussion: "How many legs does a sheep have if you call a tail a leg?" Someone in the Cabinet responded, "Well, five, of course." "Wrong!" exclaimed Lincoln. "It still has only four. *Calling a tail a leg doesn't make it one!*"

The application for us, of course, is that *calling a gay couple a family doesn't make it one!* It's just like the proverbial "rose by any other name." A traditional family by any other modern, updated definition, is still a nuclear family—with mom, dad, and their 2.3 kids.

And in that truth there is every reason not to despair. Not all the rhetoric, gay-rights laws, sensitivity training, rainbow curriculums, and stereotype-busting billboards that could ever be marshaled in aid of the gay cause will ever put an end to the traditional family. It will survive.

What we must guard against is having our own hallowed sense of family hijacked for an unworthy cause. Regardless of the trappings, sinful behavior is neither hallowed nor worthy.

That said, in the midst of all the debate over "traditional families" and "gay families," I am haunted by one disturbing thought: What kind of families did gay activists grow up in that they can't recognize the difference between the genuine and the counterfeit? What possibly could have driven them to the point where they feel they must destroy the sublime and defend the absurd? Whatever it is, that horror is more to be despised than all the gays put together who are the products of its perverted mischief.

CHAPTER 14

The Myths About Heterosexual AIDS

Sex wasn't meant to be "safe." Or negotiated. Or fatal.

—From the play *Jeffrey*,
by Paul Rudnick

The year was 1987. Oprah Winfrey dramatically opened her show, "Women Living with AIDS," with the ominous words:

> Hello, everybody. AIDS has both sexes running scared. Research studies now project that one in five—listen to me, hard to believe—one in five heterosexuals could be dead from AIDS at the end of the next three years. That's by 1990. One in five. It is no longer just a gay disease. Believe me.[1]

We are now several years beyond 1990. Not one in five, nor one in ten, nor even one in a hundred heterosexuals have died from AIDS as Oprah predicted. In fact, *not one in 3500 heterosexuals have died from AIDS!*

In just over a decade since AIDS was first diagnosed (in 1981), a total of 70,000 nongays have died from the disease, the vast majority of whom were intravenous drug abusers, followed far behind by a combination of hemophiliacs and those receiving blood transfusions infected with HIV, and a somewhat larger percentage of heterosexuals of Haitian or East African descent. What this means for heterosexuals of all categories is that, out of 250 million Americans, only .0003 percent have died in a decade from AIDS-related deaths!

It's not just Oprah, of course, who predicted the gloom. She was in good company. Teamed together with the media, the former Surgeon General C. Everett Koop had launched a campaign to "inform" America that not only was AIDS easily transmitted among heterosexuals, but that soon the "epidemic" would reach astronomical proportions.

In the same year that Oprah made her dramatic prediction, across the ocean in Great Britain the Communicable Diseases Surveillance Centre advised the Government to expect 3000 new cases (both heterosexual and homosexual) to be diagnosed in the following year. As it turned out, there were only 755 cases (predominantly homosexual). A forecast made only one year ahead was wrong by a factor of 400 percent![2]

Global predictions have been equally excessive. The U.N.'s World Health Organization (WHO) has predicted catastrophe for years among heterosexuals worldwide—a catastrophe which has yet to take place. As we will see momentarily, its predictions—focusing mainly on the continent of Africa—may have been based upon a number of false premises.

Both at home and around the globe, the coming heterosexual AIDS apocalypse has been—and for the most part continues to be—conventional wisdom. But where is the evidence? Why hasn't it happened? Did that many promiscuous heterosexuals immediately stop sleeping around? Did the panicky use of condoms bring the predicted epidemic to a screeching halt? If so, how do we account for an almost minuscule number of AIDS-related deaths resulting from the wide-open sexual activity going on in the incubation years before AIDS was discovered and the brakes put on?

It just doesn't add up. Rampant heterosexual AIDS is a myth!

You've Got a Transmission Problem

To say that heterosexual AIDS is a myth is not to say that heterosexuals can't have AIDS. Thousands of heterosexuals have AIDS or have been diagnosed as HIV-positive. As we have already seen, however, the vast majority of such heterosexuals are in the high-risk intravenous drug-abuser group. On the other hand, sadly, there are also completely innocent victims of the disease who did nothing at all to bring it on themselves. Most of these contracted AIDS through tainted blood transfusions (like tennis great Arthur Ashe) or through infections which were passed on to children by their infected mothers.

A case in point demonstrates both the good news and the bad news of heterosexual AIDS. People all across the nation were saddened to learn that Elizabeth Glaser, wife of actor/director Paul Michael Glaser (who played Starsky on the '70's detective show "Starsky and Hutch") had contracted the virus in 1981 through a blood transfusion received after giving birth to her daughter.

The bad news was compounded when she unknowingly passed the disease on to her baby, Ariel, through breast milk. Seven-year-old Ariel eventually died of AIDS complications in 1988. Their son, Jake, was also infected in utero before the Glasers knew Elizabeth was HIV-positive.

The good news is that Paul Michael never contracted the disease. And as he put it, "Until we found out that our family was infected, Elizabeth and I had a natural sexual relationship. I wasn't infected by either child, and they did everything a child can do to a parent. They bled on me, they crapped on me, they hugged me, and they kissed me. And I still don't have it."[3]

Elizabeth Glaser's Pediatric AIDS Foundation is a poignant reminder of the passivity with which HIV and AIDS can be received. In far too many cases, AIDS has walked in uninvited. To that extent, AIDS is *not* exclusively a gay disease, and deserves every effort we can make to control it.

On the other hand, we have to be careful in assessing the extent of its impact through heterosexual intercourse. Paul Michael Glaser's case tells us what any number of other studies are also showing: that AIDS is extremely difficult to get.

University of California's Nancy Padian, often referred to as the queen of partner studies because of her vast work in the field, reports that only about 20 percent of women who sleep with HIV-positive men *over a period of years* become infected. And for infection going in the other direction—from infected women to uninfected men—the figures are even less. Far less! "Of 61 HIV-positive women studied, only one transmitted the virus to her partner—and that was as a result of a highly unusual sex life."[4]

What these and other studies show is that, statistically, it is unlikely (though possible) for HIV to be transferred from a man to a woman through acts of vaginal intercourse. And the odds of it being passed from a woman to a man through vaginal intercourse are simply negligible.[5]

Further proof of the difficulty of female-to-male transmission is found in the mandatory health checks required of prostitutes in Nevada, where brothels are legal. The 32 legal brothels take in some 600,000 "dates" each year. Despite the busy traffic in heterosexual sex, *not one case* of HIV infection has been reported among the brothel's many "working girls."[6]

The reason for the relatively rare instances of people being infected through heterosexual contact is that, without some other factor being involved, there is simply a *serious transmission problem.*

How HIV Travels

The often-repeated phrase "exchange of body fluids" is itself misleading. You don't catch AIDS from toilet seats, airborne bacteria, insect bites, or even saliva or urine. That is why we have no reason to shun AIDS victims as if merely touching them will infect us. They are not lepers!

And as indicated above, normal heterosexual intercourse (and probably in most cases even oral sex) is not a good vehicle for HIV transmission. HIV, which usually (though not always) leads to AIDS, is a "blood-borne" virus. For the HIV infection to be transmitted, it must have some passage whereby it may enter the bloodstream. Without such an entry, there can be no infection.[7] Again, remember what Glaser said about his children bleeding *on* him. That kind of blood contact wasn't a threat.

What this means is that normal heterosexual intercourse (vaginal) is typically not suited to HIV transmission, whereas homosexual intercourse (anal) definitely is. With the latter, there is frequently a skin breakage that occurs during the act, usually to both parties. The same is not true of vaginal intercourse. (Sex during a woman's menstruation could possibly alter this scenario, but even then it would probably require the man to have an open lesion.)

Even where there is no skin breakage, the risks of anal intercourse are greatly enhanced because of the functional nature of the rectum. In rather simple terms, the walls of the rectum are porous, or absorbent, so that the last bit of nutrients entering the body can get into the bloodstream before being totally eliminated. That absorbency can be the HIV's best friend.

Vaginal-penile sex may be more apt to transmit HIV if the partners already have any other sexually-transmitted diseases (STD's), but this is still associated with the blood system. Sores, ulcers, and lesions caused by the STD's can open up pathways for the virus-infected semen to travel into the bloodstream.

The fact that typical HIV transmission occurs through anal intercourse explains why lesbians—although homosexuals—are almost completely unaffected by AIDS. (Female-to-female transmission has been reported in one case where "a woman infected through intravenous drug abuse appeared to have transmitted HIV to a female partner through traumatic sex practices that resulted in exposure to the blood of the drug abuser."[8]) Relative to lesbians, it can properly be said that AIDS is not a "gay disease."

Unfortunately for gay men, because of the unnatural way they have sex, AIDS is very definitely a "gay disease." Likewise, for intravenous drug-abusers AIDS is very definitely an "addict's disease." They too provide the conduit for HIV by sharing needles which inject not only drugs but also the "blood-borne" disease into their veins.

As a "gay disease," AIDS is not even the most frequent blood-borne disease affecting homosexuals. That dubious honor goes to Hepatitis B, which, being one hundred times more infectious than AIDS, kills more people in a day than AIDS does in a year.[9] According to one authority, Hepatitis B "infects the majority of homosexual men within three years of their becoming sexually active."[10]

Other False-Positive Theories

The doomsayers can be excused for having made wildly wrong predictions, because knowing what AIDS is all about has been a difficult learning process in what necessarily has been a crash course. We simply haven't understood the disease well enough, and have therefore erred on the side of caution.

One of the early misconceptions about the disease was the supposed ability of the infection to travel rapidly via sexual intercourse from one person to another and to another and to another, after first being obtained from an initial member in one of the high-risk groups. That is how other sexually-transmitted diseases (STD's), like gonorrhea and syphilis, spread.

That is what is so mystifying about HIV relative to heterosexuals. With heterosexuals, it works the exact opposite way from all other STD's. STD's thrive on multiple partners, or promiscuity. But HIV will be transmitted, if at all, only after significant sexual contact with *the same partner*.

The belief that the virus would be transmitted rapidly to distant third parties probably accounts for all the doomsday figures. But the fact is that, if such transmission happens at all, it happens only in the rare case. Virtually all cases have been members of high-risk groups and their immediate sexual partners.[11]

Enter Earvin "Magic" Johnson. I can still remember where I was and what I was doing when I first heard the broadcast. In my memory, the shocking news will always stand right up there along with President Kennedy's assassination and the explosion of the space shuttle Challenger. I was a diehard Lakers—and Magic Johnson—fan. My mind raced: "Magic has tested positive for HIV?" Like everyone else in America, I simply couldn't believe it!

Looking back, I suspect that gay activists, while struck by the tragedy like all the rest of us, had other thoughts as well, since this universally admired superstar was proof positive that even heterosexuals could get HIV. After all, hadn't Magic confessed to "accommodating as many women as possible"? What more proof could you ask for? "If it can happen to Magic, it can happen to anybody."

We may never know for sure how Magic contracted the disease. What we do know is that it's unlikely he got it through "third party" transmission. This fact suggests contact with someone in a high-risk group—in other words, blood-related contact. It galls me to even think it, but if Magic hasn't told us the whole truth about how he contracted the virus, then he has some serious apologies to make to the media, to his fans, and particularly to the young people who look up to him on the subject of AIDS.

However he got it, one simply *has* to ask why Magic's wife, Cookie, did not test HIV-positive, despite a long-standing sexual relationship with Magic. Or why we haven't had a rash of major news conferences announcing the infection of Wilt Chamberlain (who claims 20,000 sexual partners) or other NBA superstuds with similar sexual habits as Wilt and Magic.

No matter how well-intended, Magic's crusade for kids to use condoms misses the whole point. Unless they are part of some other high-risk group, their risk is not from unprotected heterosexual intercourse. Their greatest risk—ever present—is a moral risk, and not all the magic condoms in the world can spare them from its spiritual consequences.

Finally, what could prove to be a third major problem with the predictions of heterosexual AIDS is surfacing more each day in the escalating debate over whether HIV is the cause of AIDS. Several experts are beginning to question even that sacred cow. Among them, Professor Peter Duesberg, virologist at the University of California, argues that HIV itself is harmless and must be related to other factors in order for it to end up as AIDS.[12]

The coming months and years are likely to see the rise and fall of one theory after another regarding HIV and AIDS. The bottom line, however, is that at this point there is simply no evidence of widespread heterosexually transmitted infection in the United States and western Europe.

Out of Africa: More Fiction

However, if you listen to the World Health Organization and to virtually all major AIDS research bodies, you will hear a chorus of voices telling you that Africa is in the grip of a heterosexual AIDS epidemic, and that the continent is being devastated by HIV. According to WHO, we can expect half a million sub-Saharan Africans to die from AIDS each year by the turn of the century—all because of unprotected heterosexual sex.[13]

But is it true? Is the African "heterosexual AIDS" experience a dire warning to the West of what could happen to us?

Right off the bat, one would do well to consider carefully what is meant by the term *heterosexual AIDS*. As typically used, the term refers to AIDS which is acquired through heterosexual sex. That's what all the television warnings are about. That's what the neo-moralists are talking about when they encourage "safe sex" through the use of condoms.

But it is easy—especially in Africa—to get caught in the trap of saying that there is evidence of "heterosexual AIDS" (AIDS transmitted through heterosexual intercourse) simply because people who have AIDS (from whatever cause) *happen to be heterosexual*. To personalize the point, Elizabeth Glaser and her daughter Ariel are properly classified under the heading "heterosexual AIDS" (because they were both heterosexuals when they were infected); but this doesn't mean that either of them acquired the disease as a result of heterosexual sex.

Just because thousands of heterosexuals in Africa have been diagnosed as having AIDS doesn't mean that they *acquired it* through heterosexual relations.

That said, it is even more important to appreciate that just because thousands of heterosexuals in Africa *have been diagnosed as having AIDS* doesn't necessarily mean that they either actually *have* AIDS or that it was caused by HIV. Study after study is beginning to show that AIDS diagnosis in Africa is faulty on a grand scale.

Dr. Harvey Bialy, Scientific Editor of *Biotechnology*, a sister publication to the science journal *Nature*, has been visiting Africa since 1975 and has spent eight years there.[14] Dr. Bialy says that HIV tests in Africa react to non-HIV antibodies as well as to HIV itself, producing up to 80 to 90 percent false-positives. "There is vast literature showing this," he emphasizes.[15]

Even in America, it is well-known that the HIV tests can often produce false-positives, and multiple tests are recommended to confirm HIV findings. In Africa, where there is even less funding to support HIV testing, there is simply no opportunity in most cases to verify initial screening, if there is any test at all. What relatively few tests are given which indicate that the patient is HIV-positive are accepted at face value and added to the burgeoning statistics.

As suggested in the careful wording of the previous paragraph, *most AIDS diagnosis in Africa involves no HIV testing whatsoever*. Diagnosis is made on the basis of a standard Clinical Case Definition which looks at a combination of symptoms (fever, pronounced weight loss, diarrhea, and prolonged, dry cough)—all of which are virtually indistinguishable from other diseases such as malaria and tuberculosis. As a result, almost all malaria and TB cases are diagnosed today as AIDS—and so they too end up in the grim statistics.[16]

The plain fact is that "AIDS" in Africa is as likely to be related to poverty, malnutrition, inadequate medical supplies, and bad water as to HIV.

In the Ivory Coast, the relationship between AIDS and HIV is particularly suspect. In one maternity clinic in

Koumassi, for example, there is a higher incidence of HIV than in the West, but there is not a frequent progression to AIDS. At the same time, many women are classed as HIV-negative, yet they meet the definitions for AIDS![17] It suggests once again that there must be cofactors which make possible the progression from HIV to AIDS.

Among the interesting data from Uganda is another study among a hundred discordant heterosexual couples (one partner originally testing positive, the other negative). Over a two-year period, both partners became HIV-positive in only five of the couples. The significance? In 95 percent of the couples, HIV had *not* been passed on through heterosexual intercourse.[18] (That mirrors the studies already noted in the United States.)

The raw statistics alone are enough to make one sit up and take notice that something is odd indeed about the research figures coming out of Africa. Since 1984, in the West one million people have been diagnosed as having been infected with HIV, and there have been 250,000 reported cases of AIDS. In Africa during the same period, six million people have been diagnosed has having HIV, yet there are only 129,000 reported cases of AIDS.[19] How does that stack up with 1) all the horror stories about Africa, or 2) the validity of AIDS diagnosis in the dark continent?

In Tanzania, volunteers working for Partage, a French charity in aid of adoptions, asked its staff of 160 people and a whole village of 842 people to undergo HIV testing. The results were only 5 percent (among the staff) and 13.8 percent (among the villagers) who were HIV-positive. The results were *five times lower* than WHO's statistics for the region.[20]

In fact, AIDS research in Africa is severely criticized by local health officials for focusing in on some particularly chosen "epicenter" and then extrapolating the results as if they accurately represented a much larger region or even an entire nation.[21]

In this same light, Africa's prostitutes are getting a lot of attention from AIDS researchers, with their obvious potential for verifying heterosexual AIDS. And sure enough, the studies come back one after another confirming what the researchers hoped to find: a high incidence of AIDS among the prostitutes. Local health officials complain that foreign researchers pack up and leave after gathering figures for research purposes rather than assessing the figures for patient care. Hardly anyone stays around long enough to consider that the use of hard drugs among prostitutes has greatly escalated over the same period as the rise in AIDS.

According to Dr. Bialy, "The only utterly new phenomenon I have seen is in the drug-using prostitutes in Abidjan in the Ivory Coast," he said. "These girls come from Ghana, from families of prostitutes who are brought in by the busload. They have been doing this for generations, and never became sick until now."

So why now? And why do they *look like* they have AIDS? "What is new is that these girls are addicted to viciously adulterated, smokable heroin and cocaine. It completely destroys them. They look exactly like the inner-city crack-addicted prostitutes of the United States."[22] Bialy's overall conclusion about Africa and AIDS? "There is absolutely no believable, persuasive evidence that Africa is in the midst of a new epidemic of infectious immuno-deficiency."[23]

Assuming some avenue of blood transmission through one's skin, Dr. John Seale puts the prostitution issue in stark perspective: "You are more likely to get AIDS by helping an African prostitute clean up after a nose-bleed than by having sex with her."[24]

Perhaps the most compelling bit of evidence coming out of Africa is the study reported in *The Lancet* by a group of Japanese doctors. Out of a group of 227 diagnosed "AIDS" patients who had all the classic clinical signs qualifying for AIDS under the WHO definition, 59 percent showed no trace of HIV in their blood.[25]

And out of all the "AIDS cases" reported in Abidjan's three main hospitals, there were 2400 "documented" cases of AIDS that turned out not to have HIV present![26]

What's the point of this statistical parade? Simply to demonstrate that there are serious questions about the African AIDS figures which have been bandied about so glibly in America as proof of so-called "heterosexual AIDS."

Reducing Human Tragedy to Politics

And what is the point of that point in a book dealing with gay rights? Hopefully, to expose the politics of AIDS, particularly as it relates to the gay movement's cry that "AIDS is an equal-opportunity destroyer." Gay activists are concerned about the stigma that would result (at least in America) from AIDS being correctly associated primarily with homosexual behavior. The implication that they wish us to draw from the myth of heterosexual AIDS is that "we're all in it together."

If we're all equally at risk (they would have us ask ourselves), then how different can we be? If AIDS affects heterosexuals as well as homosexuals, then AIDS is not a "gay disease" and should not give anyone reason to lash out at gays for the many innocent deaths which have been caused by the disease. If AIDS is more than just a "gay disease," then it can't possibly be a sign from God that homosexual behavior is sinful. Need I go on?

Most of all, promoting AIDS as equally heterosexual helped persuade the public that any classification of homosexuals was pointless and could have no other motive than invidious discrimination.[27]

On a practical level, gay activists knew that badly needed research funds for AIDS research probably never would be received unless society felt that, as a whole, they were at risk.

And don't for a minute think that gay activists aren't aware of the enormous implications of the "heterosexual AIDS" argument. Nor that they aren't actively doing whatever it takes to keep the myth alive.

If you have any doubts, just ask Michael Fumento, former AIDS analyst for the Commission on Civil Rights. His book *The Myth of Heterosexual Aids*[28] has been the victim of censorship by the gay lobby both in America and Britain. Bookstores in New York received letters threatening boycott if they carried the book. (I can personally testify to the book's unavailability. I nearly wore out a good pair of shoes searching New York City in vain for a copy.)

The campaign to censor Fumento's book proved so successful that now even its publisher (Basic Books) has embargoed all remaining copies. You simply cannot obtain one.

In Britain, only 20 copies of Fumento's book were imported into the United Kingdom. Following gay reaction to the serialization of his book in London's *Sunday Times*, no publisher would touch it.[29] Of course, innuendos of a conspiracy were vehemently denied by Britain's publishers.

Back in the States, when *Forbes* magazine published an article favorably profiling Fumento and his views, gay activists from ACT-UP picketed the publisher's Fifth Avenue offices. The gays won a personal capitulation from Malcolm Forbes, who said that the article was "asinine," and that he would have "killed" it had he not been traveling at the time![30]

Freedom of the press? What freedom of the press? When gay rights come to town, everybody else's Constitutional rights are forced to leave. No Serbian ethnic cleansing was ever more complete. Dare question the myth of "heterosexual AIDS" and you'll have gay activists on your back before you can say "Sodom's second coming."

Putting a Price on Tragedy

Of course, it's not only the gay lobby that wants in on the action. In London, Auberon Waugh zeroes in on what he calls "the dollar dimension:"

> I wonder what persuaded the Observer this week to lead its front page with the dismal headline: "New Aids virus threatens heterosexuals". Ever since people started talking about Aids 10 years ago, medical researchers have been desperately trying to convince the world that it is a heterosexual affliction, reckoning on all the billions of dollars in research budgets which might become available.
>
> This week's scare comes from a symposium in Boston, which heard Dr. John Sullivan, of the University of Massachusetts medical centre, proclaim a global epidemic yet again. The only solution, he said, was to double biomedical research efforts and budgets. Ah yes, budgets.[31]

For researchers, grants are dependent upon the myth of heterosexual AIDS. And since the figures in the United States wouldn't even begin to be sufficiently persuasive, the scientists have turned to Africa for the supposed evidence.

Dr. Bialy says that "it has become a joke in Uganda that you are not allowed to die of anything but AIDS. A favorite story is that a friend has just been run over by a car; doctors put it down as AIDS-related suicide!"[32]

But the AIDS scare in Africa is no joke. The hysteria itself may have as serious side effects as the disease. Local health officials tell horror stories of people all over Africa who are so afraid that they will be diagnosed as having AIDS that they won't go to the hospital. And so they die at home of malaria or tuberculosis or simply malnutrition.

If fear doesn't kill them, they slowly waste away from despair. Why keep trying to live if they are going to die anyway? And everyone is telling them they are going to die.

The AIDS scare has turned families and villages against their own. Those who are diagnosed with AIDS are shunned and kicked out of the village. AIDS-infected homosexuals in America aren't the only ones who suffer from AIDS stigmatization.

It just doesn't get any more callous than when the gay lobby and the scientific community are willing to trade on the lives of others to put across their own agenda. In Uganda alone, the government has less than one dollar per person to spend on health care each year. Last year it received six million dollars in foreign funding for AIDS. What could be a greater incentive to classify people as AIDS sufferers?

But it gets worse. Of that six million, 750,000 dollars came from the World Health Organization, which at the same time gave only 57,000 dollars for the prevention and treatment of malaria, which kills an estimated one million people in sub-Saharan Africa every year.[33] Unlike AIDS, malaria is curable. But are the drugs available to do the job? No. And why? Because malaria is not a politically correct disease!

But that's still not the worst of it. The double-whammy comes when you realize that a significant number of all the reported "AIDS cases" are nothing more than curable malaria cases to begin with!

And who knows just how deceptive it gets? The World Health Organization and its colleagues in the US-AID organization are notorious for their family-planning, birth-control bias. AIDS funds go to counseling, education, and condoms—not medicine. Could there be any connection between the big budgets for condom distribution and their push for eliminating the teeming underclass in Africa?

A spokeswoman for US-AID did not deny the bias, but demurred, saying that condoms had never been the method of choice for birth control.[34] Perhaps that is true historically, but are we to believe they wouldn't take advantage of the current AIDS hysteria and kill two birds with one stone? AIDS as a political football has never been kicked in so many different directions!

Back home, those of you who are parents should also be aware that the political football is being kicked directly at your children. It's happening in the campaign to pass out condoms on school campuses all over the country. In the past, we've been able to keep the Great Condom Giveaway—with its implied moral acceptance of promiscuity—out of the classroom. Both Christian and non-Christian parents steadfastly opposed the distribution of condoms as long as the primary risk was nothing more than teenage pregnancy. (That risk has been around for a long time.) But the supposed threat of *death through AIDS* if condoms weren't used by sexually active teens was a risk that few parents were willing to take.

So now, thanks to a threat that in most communities is nothing more than a gay-promoted hoax, condoms have become as much a part of the students' wardrobe as gym shorts and Reeboks. Thanks to the immorality of *homosexual* behavior, parents and school officials have caved in to the immorality of *heterosexual* behavior.

More Callous by Comparison

If someone asked you to name a disease that is reaching crisis proportions among Americans, that often ravages people in the prime of life, that does not discriminate on grounds of race or gender, and that suffers from a lack of government funding, you would probably think of AIDS. But the correct answer, of course, is cancer.[35]

As Mona Charen reports, "In the 10 years since the AIDS epidemic began, about 120,000 Americans have died from the disease. During the same period, 40 times that many have succumbed to cancer."[36] And heart disease kills five times as many as AIDS in a single year!

To put it into perspective, AIDS-related deaths are not even in the top ten killers, but we pour more government money into AIDS than any other illness, despite its comparatively narrow impact.[37] AIDS research funding is already 10 times that of cancer on a per-death basis, and 20 times on a per-patient basis.[38] (Certainly there is no disputing that the "start-up money" has to be spent in huge sums in order to catch up with funding for other diseases where there have been years of costly research.)

Britain's figures are similarly skewed. In 1989/90, when there were 553 AIDS-related deaths, the government spent 240 million dollars on AIDS research and education. In the same year, in which 200,000 people died from heart disease, the government spent 15 million dollars for heart research. That works out to about 75 dollars for each person who died of heart disease, and 433,000 dollars for each person who died of AIDS!

In human terms, Britain's director of the Committee on Population and the Economy, Robert Whelan, reminds us that "people will die from cancer and heart disease who would not have died if additional funds had been available. Their names will never be embroidered in a quilt, and they will never be celebrated at gala entertainments. But they will die just the same."

There is no effort here to pit AIDS sufferers against those who suffer from cancer and heart disease. No one I know would begrudge the announcement that a cure for AIDS had been discovered. No one I know wouldn't wish that we could have prevented little Ariel Glaser's death. The plea here is not to cut off funding for AIDS research. The plea is that we put everything in its proper perspective.

A large part of that process is ridding ourselves of the myth of heterosexual AIDS. As Robert Whelan puts it, "After at least 30 years in the community, AIDS remains tightly confined to members of high-risk groups, such as male homosexuals and drug addicts. The much-heralded 'heterosexual explosion' has failed to materialize, despite the earnestly-expressed hopes of some workers in the AIDS field."[39]

Rather than reducing the current level of AIDS funding, society would do better to redirect where that money goes. Programs that aid intravenous drug-abusers in cities like New York desperately lack the funding necessary to deal with even a fraction of the demand for help. There is where the focus must shift. If there is any truth at all to the fears surrounding heterosexual AIDS, you can find it in the inner city.

In some areas of the south Bronx, 1 in 22 young mothers have tested positive for HIV. And what breaks your heart is that the same is true of 1 in 40 infants.[40] Naturally, the children aren't getting HIV from heterosexual intercourse, and their mothers aren't necessarily sleeping around. The mothers are either intravenous drug-abusers themselves, or have partnered on a long-term basis with a man who is. In high-risk-group communities like the south Bronx, the escalation of AIDS among heterosexuals promises to be a continuing serious threat. For those who are caught up in a culture of cocaine and crack addiction, every penny spent on prevention of drug abuse and on AIDS research is well worth the investment.

When it comes to the highest-risk group of all, however, in the long range *absolutely no public funding is needed or warranted*. Finding a cure for those already infected is one thing. Let's do it if we can, as soon as we can. But *preventing* AIDS-related deaths among homosexual males is not a matter of medical research. Common sense tells you that, if AIDS results primarily from anal intercourse, then the solution ought to be obvious! No, not condoms, but homosexual abstinence.

In 1986/87, the taxpayer-funded National Centers for Disease Control made two grants totaling almost 675,000 dollars to the Gay Men's Health Crisis, Inc. of New York, following its proposal to spend the money in part upon a manual for conducting "Eroticizing Safer Sex Workshops." According to the grant application, the workshops were intended to "discover and share information on how to be sexually active in low-risk ways."[41]

Taxpayer-funded programs to educate gays about AIDS is a sick joke. No group of individuals knows better how AIDS is transmitted than male homosexuals. Why else do they "negotiate" safe sex? (They don't even have the excuse of addicts that their perception is so altered by drugs that they can't put two and two together.) And this gets us to the heart of the matter: What gays really want is *risk-free sodomy*!

Gays don't want to stop their homosexual behavior— only to pressure the government into discovering the equivalent of "the pill" for males wishing to have intercourse with each other. And then when "the pill"— whatever in the future it might turn out to be—happens to fail, they want the rest of us to foot the bill for hospitalization. At the present time, the cost of treating the average AIDS patient from diagnosis to death is 100,000 dollars.

And, of course, the quicker the government can discover a medical means of prevention, the better. But the money/time factor itself is nonsense. You get the idea among many gay activists that if twice as much money is spent on the AIDS budget, then the disease will be cured twice as fast. That if three times as much is spent, then the cure will come three times as fast. But medical research doesn't work that way. If it did, we probably would have beaten cancer and heart disease by now.[42]

For homosexual males, AIDS is a self-inflicted fatality. If they want a speedy end to the crisis, it is within their own power to make it happen. (Proof of that is the statistical plateau that apparently has already been reached in the incidence of AIDS among homosexuals.) Playing on the fears of heterosexuals (and jumping the cue to get ahead of those who suffer from other diseases) in order to continue their self-destructive behavior is a callous game indeed.

Our Own Mismanagement of AIDS

One of the grand ironies of the myth of heterosexual AIDS is that it has been widely perpetuated by the Christian community. It is just one more way in which we have mismanaged the entire AIDS affair. We hurt our credibility from the very start by saying that AIDS was a plague from God specifically to single out and punish homosexuals. We didn't stop to think that lesbians were left untouched by the plague; or that many innocents were also plagued, or that the figures for white homosexuals and homosexuals from other ethnic groups were often greatly disparate. It should have been enough to say that sin always has built-in consequences, often *physical* consequences.

But turning around and virtually arguing against ourselves, we took up the gay movement's banner of heterosexual AIDS in order to denounce heterosexual promiscuity as well. Proclaiming the widespread heterosexual nature of the epidemic as fervently as any gay activists, we (rightly) called for sexual abstinence and monogamous, married sex. And with that proclamation in aid of a biblical cause, we played directly into the hands of the gay lobby. How they must have snickered behind our backs!

Ironically, the same Michael Fumento who angered the gays by daring to suggest that the AIDS focus ought to be on high-risk homosexuals was demoted from his position as AIDS analyst for the Reaganesque Commission on Civil Rights because he suggested that the religious and conservative right were also manipulating the AIDS crisis to their own ends. Can the Christian community not face up to self-criticism?

It must be asked, What did we gain by jumping on the gay's "heterosexual AIDS" bandwagon? Morality by fear? The previously promiscuous heterosexual who gives up sex in order to avoid AIDS is not suddenly more moral—just more practical! Although the words look very much alike, there is a vast spiritual gulf between being *sacred* and being *scared*.

Can we not see that, in using heterosexual AIDS as an argument against extramarital sex, we run the risk of having no moral persuasion left should the time come (and it likely will) when some medical prevention or cure for AIDS is discovered? Why make morality so vulnerable to science? The moral issue can, and should, stand on its own.

Whatever the issue, pragmatism is never good theology. With the myth of "heterosexual AIDS," good theology has not even been truly pragmatic. It is not the *myth* that we should perpetuate, but the *message*.

CHAPTER 15

Manifesto for Sexual Sanity

Once to every man and nation comes the moment
*   to decide,*
In the strife of Truth with Falsehood, for the good
*   or evil side....*
                                    —James Russell Lowell

The reporter who spent more time with Bill Clinton than did any other on the campaign was Mark Miller, 29, of *Newsweek*. Miller is openly gay, and Clinton knows it. In Las Vegas a year ago, Miller, Clinton, and several aides were being driven by a Nevada state trooper. Someone in the car pointed out an attractive woman on the street. While others agreed, Miller responded, "Not bad. I wonder if she has a brother?"

As reported by Adam Nagourney in *The New Republic*, the state trooper's head spun around, and Clinton burst out laughing. "Clinton tells that story all the time," Miller says now. "He thinks it's one of the funniest things."[1]

America is going to hell in a hatbox and our President is laughing about it. The mystery is that so many people in the Christian community helped vote him into office. Though God is not a Republican, Bill Clinton's official stance on such moral issues as abortion and gay rights was simply too public to be ignored. (Were Christians more concerned with economics than morality?)

One wonders if God isn't giving America what it asked for. When the people of Israel wanted a king like the nations around them, God reluctantly gave them a king. Not until it was too late did the people realize that their king was not to be the benevolent sovereign that the King of Heaven had been. When king after king led God's people into spiritual decline and political ruin, it was too late to complain.[2]

It's time we Christians asked some hard questions. How close are we getting to the brink? How much sand is left in the hourglass for America?

If there is any hope at all, apart from the grace of God itself, it may be the current shift in the political landscape. Ironically, gays actually may have lost ground. As long as there was a President who was willing to take a stand against gay activists (whether his motivation was a matter of personal conviction or was merely politically shaped), gays could claim the position of underdog. They could always be viewed as victims of political conservatives and the religious right. But now that there is a President who is on their side, the sympathy vote for gays actually may have backfired.

Now, more than ever, it's time for Christians to step forward and take the initiative. The political battle lines are already set. In the months ahead, ballot propositions will test the issues in at least a dozen states, including California, Georgia, Idaho, Iowa, Maine, Michigan, Minnesota, Missouri, Montana, Ohio, Oregon, and Washington. (Gay activists are striking back with their own well-financed coalition. They not only plan to counter grassroots measures in each state, but also to go on the offensive, accelerating the passage of pro-gay legislation.)

Taking the Initiative

Colorado's Amendment 2, which passed in November

1992 by a margin of 54 to 46 percent, has already been put on hold by the courts. On this issue, the will of the people hardly seems to matter. The beauty of Amendment 2 was its simplicity in response to gay-rights ordinances in various Colorado cities. The text of the amendment is worth reading:

> Neither the State of Colorado, through any of its branches or departments, nor any of its agencies, political subdivisions, municipalities or school districts, shall enact, adopt or enforce any statute, regulation, ordinance or policy whereby homosexual, lesbian or bisexual orientation, conduct, practices or relationships shall constitute or otherwise be the basis of or entitle any person or class of persons to have or claim any minority status quota preferences, protected status or claim of discrimination.

The language of Amendment 2 is significant because there is nothing vitriolic about it. It doesn't require voters to make any kind of moral pronouncement about homosexual orientation or behavior, but simply prohibits any special legislation in favor of gays. Middle America can buy that kind of legislation.

By way of contrast, the language of Oregon's Proposition 9, in the same year, called for voters to demand that affirmative steps be taken by the state to actively encourage anti-gay attitudes:

> (1) This state shall not recognize any categorical provision such as "sexual orientation" and "sexual preference," and similar phrases that include homosexuality, pedophilia, sadism or masochism. Quotas, minority status, affirmative action, or any similar concepts,

shall not apply to any form of conduct, nor shall the government promote these behaviors.

(2) State, regional and local governments and their properties and monies shall not be used to promote, encourage, or facilitate homosexuality, pedophilia, sadism or masochism.

(3) State, regional, and local governments, and their departments, agencies and other entities, including specifically the State Department of Higher Education, and the public schools, shall assist in setting a standard for Oregon's youth that recognizes homosexuality, pedophilia, sadism, or masochism as abnormal, wrong, unnatural, and perverse and that these behaviors are to be discouraged and avoided.

In drafting that language, the Oregon Citizens Alliance was responding to polls in their state which indicated voters were hesitant to "discriminate" against gays, but did have great concern for what might happen to their children in the classroom. Hence the more proactive approach which has received criticism from some quarters. However, because other factors were involved, it would be impossible to judge exactly what impact the different approach may have had on the outcome. (Proposition 9 garnered 44 percent of the vote.)

Not the least of the possible reasons for Proposition 9's defeat was the dollar factor. While "Yes on 9" supporters spent 500,000 dollars, the pro-gay "No on 9" backers spent an unbelievable 2.5 million dollars! (In Colorado, by comparison, Amendment 2 was backed by 400,000 dollars and opposed by 700,000 dollars.)

And who's to know what impact the state's leading newspaper, *The Oregonian*, may have had through its editorial blitz against Prop 9? Just imagine 27 negative editorials in 60 days, including 12 in a row! On the day before the vote, the publisher of *The Oregonian*, Fred Stickel, wrote a personal editorial slamming Prop 9, for which he was later given an award by the "No on 9" forces at (where else) an ACLU banquet.

It wasn't only the secular press. The Archbishop of Portland, William J. Lavada, also came out against Proposition 9. While acknowledging that "sexual orientation" by itself does not constitute a quality comparable to race or ethnic background as a basis for guaranteeing civil rights, the archbishop nevertheless wavered:

> But we think it important to ensure that our discussion and our legislation about the increasingly public issues related to homosexuality be accomplished through a process of civic dialogue which avoids caricature and over-dramatization on either side, which can so easily feed the residual hates and discrimination which are our sad inheritance as Americans.[3]

Without second-guessing the validity of what is obviously a sincere evaluation made regarding Proposition 9's particular wording, it is the second time we've seen an archbishop making what, to gays, would appear to be a concession. As mentioned before, it is an almost inconceivable thought: Can it really be that the Catholic Church is showing signs of fracture in what was once a united front against the homosexual lobby?

In November of 1994, Oregon will once again be the battleground for another anti-gay proposition, this time with a modified version of Proposition 9. Philip Ramsdell, a spokesman for the Oregon Citizens Alliance, is excited about the possibilities for success the next time around. "Other states are going to be looking to Oregon for model legislation," he predicted.[4]

Whatever approaches may be used, fighting gay rights is going to require the very sharpest skills of legal analysis and political wit. My own experience as a supporter of California's Proposition 6 back in 1978—the so-called "gay teacher" initiative—taught me a lesson or two about the pitfalls of moral-issue politics. The most important lesson was that it is virtually impossible to avoid a boomerang ballot. With the liberal press biased against moral concerns, and with opponents whose immoral standards can justify deviant behavior not only in the bedroom but in politics, a just cause hardly stands a chance. No matter how carefully ballot language is crafted, you can be sure that gay-rights activists are going to make it into something it's not.

California's Proposition 6, for example, would have given school boards the power to dismiss any teacher "advocating, soliciting, imposing, encouraging, or promoting any private or public homosexual activity directed at or likely to come to the attention of school children and/or other school employees." It did not restrict private homosexual conduct on the part of any teacher. But how was the issue subsequently framed by gay activists and the press? As an initiative requiring the firing of any teacher who happened to be gay, no matter how private his or her sex life! The voters turned in a predictable defeat.

Jesus might just as well have been talking directly to us when he told his disciples, "I am sending you out like sheep among wolves. Therefore be as shrewd as snakes and as innocent as doves."[5] In dealing with the gay movement, we must indeed be shrewd, wise, and discerning, for we can expect nothing but political perversion.

I find it quite encouraging that in the immediately preceding verse Jesus made reference to Sodom and Gomorrah and to God's judgment against them. Speaking of any other city which would reject Christ's teaching (could it be San Francisco, West Los Angeles, or Key West?), Jesus said, "I tell you the truth, it will be more bearable for Sodom and Gomorrah on the day of judgment than for that town."[6]

Taking Stock of Our Attitude

But if we are shrewd, wise, and discerning relative to the issues involved, we must also be as innocent and harmless as doves in how we conduct ourselves in the fight. Ours will be the moral high ground only so long as we live our lives to exemplify Christ and to manifest an attitude that is consistent with the cause. "Speaking the truth in love"[7] is still the banner. "Love your enemies"[8] is still the challenge.

When I think of Christ's call for us to be innocent, harmless, and gentle, I think of a man whose gentle spirit was the strength behind Colorado's Amendment 2. He isn't a church leader as such, nor someone with a political power base in the Rockies. Will Perkins is simply a humble servant with a heart for God.

A resident of Colorado Springs, Will Perkins has been a retailer of automobiles since 1946. In addition to his dealership, Perkins Motor Company, Will is widely known and respected in the Christian community. He is a member of the Village Seven Presbyterian Church, where he has worked in the evangelism program for over 20 years. For over 30 years he has been a member of the Christian Businessmen's Committee. But here is what I like best about Will Perkins. At appropriate times during the year, Will pulls his auto commercials and airs instead some simple pleas to the viewing public to come to know Jesus Christ.

When gay rights reared its ugly head in Colorado, Will stepped forward and took on the challenge. As Chairman of the Board of Colorado for Family Values, he led a coalition of concerned citizens to the successful passage of Amendment 2. And, of course, Will Perkins is only one among many who have been in the front lines of the battle in Colorado, Oregon, and all across the nation.

I think it is important for us to know some of the people behind the scenes of the fight against gay rights. They are not radicals or right-wing Nazis. They are not homophobes. They are godly husbands and fathers, wives and mothers—all solid citizens who are simply concerned about the unrighteousness sweeping our country. And don't think that Will and others in the forefront of the battle haven't paid a price. Who ever would have believed that Christians in Colorado would be characterized (in the words of one pro-gay advocate) as "social pollutants"! Does not that libelous characterization speak volumes about how close we have come to the brink of moral anarchy?

Counting the Cost

For over 200 years we have been blessed with religious peace and freedom like no nation before us. Never have we as Christians truly had to face persecution in our own country. But we have no assurance that this peace will long continue. In fact, the time of our testing has clearly arrived. It's not only sneers and jeers that are now coming our way, but physical harm as well.

Nothing could be more characteristic of radical gay activists than threats and violence. The gay movement is not your average political action committee. Within its ranks are those who have no regard for anyone else's freedom, or privacy, or even physical safety. Just look what happens when the gay gestapo is around: The Governor of California has eggs thrown at him when he vetoes gay-rights legislation. Windows are shattered and buildings are destroyed when gays don't get what they want. In Oregon, the office of the Oregon Citizens Alliance receives what the attached ominous note says is

HIV-infected human feces. Police must guard the school buses on which the children of OCA officials are riding; and OCA president Lon Mahon has to wear a bulletproof vest because of threats to his life.

To be on the receiving end of this kind of treatment, you don't even have to be a Christian activist. Journalist Leslie Kaufman chronicles some of the furor over Michael Fumento's book on AIDS in an article entitled "Beat the Press—Death threats and bullying tactics follow AIDS journalists who contradict the conventional wisdom":

> Soon after *Newsday* published a book review by Michael Fumento, the newspaper's book editor, Jack Schwartz, began receiving anonymous phone calls late at night. Nasty calls. "They made a lot of threats," Schwartz recalls, "not the least of which was death." The calls came seven or eight a night for a month. It was clear very few of the callers had actually read the review, says Schwartz.
>
> Not long after the review appeared, Schwartz was "zapped." That is, his name and phone number were published in large, bold type in *Outweek*. The angry commentary that accompanied the number and invited readers to share their rage with Schwartz ran: "Why the _____ would *Newsday* have such a hate-filled, untalented, lying loser review important books?"[9]

Jack Schwartz was not alone. Gina Kolata, a science writer for *The New York Times*, also became the target of a vicious campaign in 1990 in the wake of her story about why so many health-care professionals objected to the liberalized distribution of experimental AIDS drugs. Shortly thereafter, bumper stickers appeared on *Times* newsboxes around New York City, saying: "Gina Kolata of the New York Times is the Worst AIDS Reporter in America." Not terribly catchy, but there was no mistaking the message.

In addition, ACT-UP members complained to Kolata's editors and colleagues that she was incompetent, and—lowering the level considerably—they sent Kolata several hundred angry, threatening Christmas cards.[10]

It's the same song, third verse, for *The Albany Times Union's* Daniel Lynch, who dared suggest in one of his columns that the media had exaggerated the threat of AIDS. His offense was in confessing his amazement at a Gallup poll which reported that Americans identified AIDS as the greatest health threat to the country, when in actuality AIDS is the number 11 killer, behind cancer, diabetes, and even liver disease. For expressing that politically incorrect opinion, Lynch was rewarded with a truckload of less-than-solicitous mail, hostile and violent callers on talk shows, and a major advertiser demanding that Lynch's column be pulled.[11]

All of this is to say that those who dare take a stand for what is moral on the issue of gay rights are likely to encounter a response from the gay movement of a type which we have never had to face before. As daunting as that prospect is, at least it puts us in good company with Jesus' disciples, to whom he said:

> Be on your guard against men; they will hand you over to the local councils and flog you in their synagogues. On my account you will be brought before governors and kings as witnesses to them and to the Gentiles.[12]

> All men will hate you because of me, but he who stands firm to the end will be saved.[13]

> Do not be afraid of those who kill the body but cannot kill the soul. Rather, be afraid of the One who can destroy both soul and body in hell.[14]

And, of course, we have the example of Jesus himself, who time and again experienced the pain of persecution and finally suffered a cruel death at the hands of his tormentors. Should we think that there is no time at which we too must know what it means to stand boldly in the face of persecution?

A Moral Manifesto

In the battle against gay rights, we must resolve to counter the gay's 12-step agenda, step-by-step. Their agenda—reversed and rebutted—must become our own manifesto:

1. Boldly reject the homosexuals' claims of freedom from social restraint and take the initiative in fostering adherence to God's moral order.

2. Refuse to give homosexuals legitimacy through claimed association with legitimate minorities and causes.

3. Show individual homosexuals so much love that no one could ever justly accuse us of being homophobic or homohaters.

4. Spread the word that the "10-percent gay" figure is nothing but gay propaganda, but let it also be known that preference for the gay lifestyle is on the increase.

5. Make sure that the public knows the difference between sexual orientation and sexual behavior, and oppose all legislation using "orientation" as a guise for homosexual behavior.

6. Be on guard against bogus claims for some genetic cause for homosexual behavior, and press medical researchers on the validity of their claims.

7. Let the whole world know what it is that gays actually do sexually, and never dignify that which is degrading even to the people who engage in it.

8. Reassert what the Bible teaches about homosexual conduct, and challenge pro-gay theologians when they distort the clear meaning of scriptural prohibitions against homosexual behavior.

9. Educate the church on the movement for gay rights and lovingly confront any pastors and evangelists who take a soft line on the issue.

10. Lobby legislators and politicians not to loosen legal restrictions against sodomy, and organize opposition to any proposed special rights legislation for gays.

11. Oppose any efforts to allow homosexuals to marry or to adopt children, and fight in every way possible for preservation of traditional family values.

12. Spread the word about how heterosexual AIDS has become a propaganda ploy to shift the focus from the gay's own immoral conduct, and, wherever possible, counter the condom lobby.

A Call to Arms

Now that we have had a frank talk about gay rights, it is time we moved from mere talk to fervent prayer and purposeful action. If you haven't written a letter to your congressman, do so—and also write to your state legislators and city council members. (Maybe you will want to send along your copy of this book.) Letters to the editor in your local paper can also help shape public opinion. But write your letters carefully and prayerfully. The last thing we need is to have a barrage of misinformation or strident diatribes coming from the Christian community.

Focus your letters on: 1) the recent studies showing the number of practicing gays to be from 1 to 3 percent of the population instead of the mythical 10 percent; 2) the lack of proof for any biological or genetic cause for homosexual orientation; 3) the gays' own admission that homosexual behavior is a matter of choice, as indicated by their frequent use of "sexual preference" and "gay lifestyle"; 4) the fact that, under gay-rights legislation, gay couples would be given greater rights than unmarried heterosexual couples and than virtually anyone else in the areas of housing and employment; and 5) how gay rights almost always means the curtailment of religious rights specifically guaranteed by the Constitution.

It's a judgment call, but parading a long list of Scriptures before a society which no longer respects the Bible may be counterproductive—a modern instance of "casting pearls before swine." The good news is that, because morality and the Scriptures go hand in hand, we can take the moral high ground without being slanderously stereotyped as mindless Bible-thumpers. Where circumstances invite, however, we must not sidestep the issue. The world needs to be reminded again and again that, through His written Word, God has condemned homosexual conduct. It's not just our own biases or prejudices that call us to oppose it.

At church, encourage your minister to speak out on the subject of homosexual behavior. And perhaps your Sunday school class or midweek Bible study can explore the issues in even more depth. Talk with young people about gay rights and help them learn how to be sensitive to those who struggle with a homosexual orientation, while at the same time drawing a clear line on homosexual behavior itself. Help them have the courage to counter the social pressure to be nonjudgmental to the point of condoning sin. It's the next generation's resolve that will tell the tale.

Whatever else you may do, open your eyes fully to the spiritual battle that is taking place in our homes, schools, businesses, legislative halls, and even the White House. If militant gays win the battle for America's hearts and minds, our nation may have crossed the Rubicon, never again to honor God.

Gay rights is not just another political issue. Nor is it just another moral issue. Gay rights presents us with the ultimate issue of our time: Whether or not God will ever again be honored in our nation. For Christians, the issue is a call to arms. For those who trust in God, it is a call to prayer.

> *God of grace, show us mercy. Give us unwavering hearts in the midst of a nation which threatens to turn its back on You. Lead us in truth; lead us in love. And most of all, lead us in paths of righteousness for Your own name's sake.*

Notes

Chapter 1—Gays at Your Doorstep
1. Denise Hamilton, "Colleges, ROTC Confront Gays in Military Issue," in *Los Angeles Times*, Sep. 20, 1993, A3.
2. 1 Peter 3:15.
3. Romans 1:27.
4. Robert Williams, *Just As I Am* (New York: Crown, 1992), p. 98.
5. Genesis 19:1-28; Jude 7.
6. Numbers 25:1-9; 1 Corinthians 10:7,8.

Chapter 2—The Not-So-Hidden Gay Agenda
1. E. Rueda, *Homosexual Network* (Greenwich, CN: Devin-Adair Publishers, 1982), pp. 202-03.
2. John 8:34.
3. Marshall Kirk and Hunter Madsen, *After the Ball* (New York: Plume, 1990), p. 188.
4. Ibid., p. 52.
5. *Boston Globe*, January 6, 1993, LIVING, p. 28.
6. Waldman, "Battle," p. 42.
7. Bob Dart, "Activists see this decade as the 'gay 90's,'" Cox News Service, Feb. 1993.
8. Martin Kasindorf, "Clinton isn't marching but is in step with gays," *The Nashville Banner*, Apr. 23, 1993,p. A1.
9. Kirk and Madsen, *After the Ball*, p. 47.
10. Ibid.
11. Frank Johnson, "Of Militants and the Military," in the *Daily Telegraph*, Feb. 3, 1993, p. 17.
12. Ibid.

Chapter 3—Homophobia and Other Finger-Pointing
1. Kirk and Madsen, *After the Ball*, p. 111.
2. Kirk and Madsen, *After the Ball*, p. xxiv.
3. See William K. Jensen in the Eugene, Oregon, *Register-Guard*, Oct. 25, 1992. Complete text adapted with permission.
4. Charles J. Sykes, *A Nation of Victims* (New York: St. Martin's Press, 1992), p. 166.
5. Ibid.
6. Carnegie Foundation for the Advancement of Teaching, *Campus Life: In Search of Community*, 1990, p. 19.
7. "Taking Offense," in *Newsweek*, Dec. 24, 1990.
8. John 8:44.
9. John 8:48.

Chapter 4—Ten Percent Gay: The Big Lie
1. Patrick Rogers, "How Many Gays Are There?" in *Newsweek*, Feb. 15, 1993, Society, p. 46.
2. Stephen Green, *The Sexual Dead-End* (London: Broadview Books, 1992), p. 61.
3. Rogers, "How Many Gays?"
4. Kirk and Madsen, *After the Ball*, p. 46.
5. Marian Faux, *Roe v. Wade* (New York: Macmillan Publishing, 1988), p. 26.
6. Rogers, "How Many Gays?"
7. Ibid.
8. Lynette Burrows, "Sunday comment," in *The Sunday Telegraph*, p. 20.
9. Jeff Lyon, "Keeping Score," in the *Chicago Tribune*, Nov. 29, 1992, Sunday Magazine, p. 14.
10. Burrows, "Sunday comment."
11. Rogers, "How Many Gays?"
12. Ibid.
13. "All Things Considered," National Public Radio, Apr. 15, 1993, findings published in *Journal for Family Planning Perspectives*, Dr. John Billy and Albert Klassen.
14. Information provided by the Centers for Disease Control and Prevention, as of Mar. 10, 1993.
15. Ibid.

Chapter 5—The Confusing War of Words
1. 1 Corinthians 2:11.
2. Leviticus 18:19; 20:18.
3. Genesis 2:18.
4. Steve Sternberg, "AIDS in China," in *The Atlanta Journal and Constitution*, Mar. 24, 1991, Foreign News, Section A, p. 9.
5. Isaiah 5:20.
6. Genesis 3:4.

Chapter 6—Can a Homosexual Change His Spots?
1. Shirley MacLaine, *Out On a Limb* (New York: Bantam Books, 1983) p. 199.
2. Kirk and Madsen, *After the Ball*, p. 35.

3. David Gelman, "Born or Bred?" in *Newsweek*, Feb. 24, 1992, p. 38.
4. Kim Painter, "Studying the Nature of Being Gay," in *USA Today*, March 8, 1993, LIFE, p. 1D.
5. Kurt Chandler, "New Studies Explore Roots of Homosexuality," in the *Star Tribune*, Dec. 6, 1992, Metro Edition, p. 12.
6. Joe Dallas, "Born Gay?" in *Christianity Today*, June 22, 1992, p. 20.
7. Gelman, "Born or Bred?" p. 40.
8. Darrell Yates Rist, "Are Homosexuals Born That Way?" in *The Nation*, Oct. 19, 1992, Vol. 255, No. 12, p. 424.
9. Maugh, "Survey of Identical Twins Links Biological Factors with Being Gay," in the *Los Angeles Times*, Sunday, Dec. 15, 1991, Home Edition, Part A, p. 43.
10. Ibid.
11. Dallas, "Born Gay?" p. 22.
12. Gelman, "Born or Bred?" p. 44.
13. Neville Hodgkinson, "Gender Bender?", in *The Sunday Times*, London, July 18, 1993, p. 12.
14. Ibid.
15. Ibid.
16. Richard Dawkins, "It's not all in the genes," in *The Daily Telegraph*, July 17, 1993, p. 14.
17. Roger J. Magnuson, *Are Gay Rights Right?* (Portland, OR: Multnomah, 1990), p. 22.
18. Ibid.
19. Gelman, "Born or Bred?" p. 41.
20. Kirk and Madsen, *After the Ball*, p. 32.
21. Joe Dallas, *Desires in Conflict* (Eugene, OR: Harvest House Publishers, 1991), p. 10.
22. Ibid., p. 11.
23. Ibid., p. 92.
24. Ibid., p. 94.
25. Gelman, "Born or Bred?" p. 41.
26. 1 Corinthians 6:9,10.
27. 1 Corinthians 6:11.
28. 1 Corinthians 6:9.
29. 1 Corinthians 6:12.
30. Gelman, "Born or Bred?" p. 44.
31. Jeremiah 6:13-15.

Chapter 7—Lesbians and Playboys: Disoriented Sex

1. Hayden Curry and Denis Clifford, *A Legal Guide for Lesbian and Gay Couples* (Berkeley: Nolo Press, 1991), 7:5.
2. Gelman, "Born or Bred?" p. 40.
3. Ibid.
4. Ibid.
5. Gelman, "Born or Bred?" p. 40.
6. Painter, "Studying the Nature," p. 1D.
7. Ibid.
8. Elizabeth Mehren, "A Place to Call Home," in the *Los Angeles Times*, Dec. 19, 1991, p. E1.
9. Ibid., p. E12.
10. Ibid., p. E1.
11. Ibid.
12. Elizabeth Mehren, "Smith Faces Up to Its Reputation on Sexuality," in the *Los Angeles Times*, Dec. 19, 1991, p. E14.
13. Ibid., p. E12.
14. Angela Phillips and Jill Rakusen, *The New Our Bodies Ourselves* (London: Penguin, 1989).
15. Ibid., p. 192.
16. Ibid.
17. Ibid., p. 209.
18. Ibid.
19. Ibid., p. 213.
20. Ibid., p. 193.
21. Ibid., p. 208.
22. Ibid., p. 204.
23. *New Dimensions*, Oct. 1990, p. 42.
24. James Dalrymple, "Anger over US don's support for paedophiles," in the London *Sunday Times*, Mar. 7, 1993; and John Carey, "The Age of Innocents," in the London *Sunday Times*, Mar. 7, 1993, BOOKS, p. 8.
25. Charles Laurence, "Playboy chief admits to being bisexual," in the London *Daily Telegraph*, Mar. 13, 1993, p. 1.
26. Ibid.
27. Sternberg, "Aids in China," p. 9.
28. Genesis 19:4.
29. William Barclay, *The Letters to the Corinthians*, Rev. Ed. (Philadelphia: Westminster Press, 1975), pp. 53, 54.
30. Rist, "Born?" p. 424.

Chapter 8—The Dark Side of Being Gay

1. Kirk and Madsen, *After the Ball*, p. 187.
2. Ibid.

3. Green, *Dead End*, p. 74.
4. Joe Brewer, "Conflict on Castro," in *The Gay Times*, Mar. 1988, p. 44.
5. Waldman, "Battle," p. 42.
6. Green, *Dead End*.
7. Pat Califia in Daniel Tsang, ed., "The Age Taboo," Alyson Publications and Gay Men's Press, 1981, p. 144.
8. "Understanding Paedophilia," PIE Vol. 1, No. 3, Aug./Sep. 1977, p. 4.
9. Michael J. Ybarra, "Going Straight: Christian Groups Press Gay People to Take a Heterosexual Path," in *The Wall Street Journal*, Apr. 21, 1993, p. A1.
10. Gay Liberation Front Manifesto, p. 9.
11. Isabel Wilkerson in *New York Times*, Oct. 18, 1990, Late Edition Final, Sec. C, p. 17.
12. Ibid.
13. Ibid.
14. David Eberly, "Homophobia, Censorship, and the Arts," in Warren J. Blumenfeld, ed., *Homophobia, How We All Pay the Price* (Boston: Beacon Press, 1992), p. 215.
15. "Hollywood Experiences Political Clout in 1992," in Showbiz Today, CNN, Dec. 28, 1992.
16. Richard Dorment, "A vile talent to disturb," in *The Daily Telegraph*, Mar. 17, 1993, p. 22.
17. Ibid.
18. Psalm 51:2,3,7.

Chapter 9—Scripturephobic Bible-Bashing
1. Williams, *Just As I Am*, p. 39.
2. Ibid., p. 54.
3. Elisabeth Schussler Fiorenza, *Bread Not Stone: The Challenge of Feminist Biblical Interpretation* (Boston: Beacon Press, 1984), p. xiii.
4. James H. Cone, *God of the Oppressed* (New York: Seabury Press, 1975), p. 37.
5. Dorothee Solle, *Beyond Mere Obedience*, translation of *Phantasie und Gehorsam*, Lawrence W. Denef, trans. (Minneapolis: Augsburg, 1970), pp. 30ff.
6. Williams, *Just As I Am*, p. 26.
7. Ibid., p. 56.
8. Ibid., p. 58.
9. Ibid., pp. 116-17.
10. Ezekiel 16:49.
11. Ezekiel 16:50.
12. Williams, *Just As I Am*, p. 48.
13. Jude 7.
14. 2 Peter 2:6-8.
15. Williams, *Just As I Am*, p. 50.
16. Leviticus 11:12.
17. Deuteronomy 7:25.
18. Deuteronomy 17:1.
19. Deuteronomy 18:12.
20. Deuteronomy 24:4.
21. Proverbs 6:17.
22. Williams, *Just As I Am*, p. 42.
23. Ibid., p. 53.
24. Ibid.
25. Ibid., p. 51.
26. Margaret A. Farley, "Feminist Consciousness and the Interpretation of Scripture," in Letty M. Russell, ed., *Feminist Interpretation of the Bible* (Philadelphia: Westminster Press, 1985), p. 43.
27. Williams, *Just As I Am*, p. 52.
28. Ibid., p. xvi.
29. Ibid., p. xii.
30. Ibid., p. 87.
31. Ibid., p. 91.
32. Ibid.
33. Ibid., p. 92.
34. Ibid., p. 150.
35. Ibid., p. 172.
36. Matthew 19:14.
37. Matthew 18:6,7.

Chapter 10—Will the Church Sell Out?
1. Matthew 7:9-11.
2. John 16:13.
3. 2 Timothy 3:16,17.
4. F. LaGard Smith, *The Cultural Church* (Nashville, TN: 20th Century Christian, 1992), Chapter 13, "The Deafening Roar of Biblical Silence."
5. Habakkuk 2:20.
6. Romans 1:25.
7. Jude 3.
8. Matthew 19:6.
9. James R. Edwards, "Eros Deified," in *Christianity Today*, May 27, 1991, pp. 14-15.
10. Mike McManus, "Presbyterians soundly reject proposals on sexuality," in the *Abilene Reporter-News*, Sunday, June 16, 1991, p. 14.

11. Ibid.
12. Damian Thompson, "Carey threat sinks plan for homosexual prayer book," in *The Daily Telegraph*, Nov. 10, 1992.
13. "Daring to Speak Love's Name," in *The Sunday Times* (London), Nov. 8, 1992.
14. Williams, *Just As I Am*, p. 231.
15. Ibid., p. 232.
16. 1 Timothy 4:1-4.
17. Williams, *Just As I Am*, pp. 228-29.
18. Ibid., p. xv.
19. *Los Angeles Times*, Feb. 13, 1993, Home Ed., Part A, p. 1.

Chapter 11—Storming the Courts for Gay Rights
1. *Bowers v. Hardwick*, 478 U.S. 186 (1968).
2. Gerard V. Bradley, "The Constitution and the Erotic Self," in *First Things*, Oct. 1991, No. 16, p. 28.
3. Bettina Boxall, "L.A.'s New Gay Muscle," in the *Los Angeles Times Magazine*, Mar. 28, 1993, p. 28.
4. Ibid.
5. Ibid.
6. Ibid.
7. Margaret L. Usdansky, "Gay couples, by the numbers," in *USA Today*, Apr. 12, 1993, pp. 1A, 8A.
8. Boxall, "Muscle."
9. Ibid.
10. Magnuson, *Are Gay Rights Right?*, p. 71.
11. 156 *California Reporter* 14 (1979).

Chapter 12—It's an All-Out Cultural War
1. David A. J. Richards, *Sexual Autonomy and the Constitutional Right to Privacy: A Case Study in Human Rights and the Unwritten Constitution*, 30 Hastings L. J. 957 (1979) at 1005.
2. Robert H. Bork, *The Tempting of America* (New York: The Free Press, 1990), p. 124.
3. Terence Shaw, "Homosexuals who agreed to torture lose legal battle," in *The Daily Telegraph*, Mar. 12, 1993, p. 10.
4. Neil Darbyshire, "Theatre director died during bizarre sex act," in *The Daily Telegraph*, Mar. 12, 1993, p. 10.
5. Henry Weinstein, "Rental Denial Is Upheld on Religious Basis," in the *Los Angeles Times*, Nov. 28, 1991, p. A34.
6. Green, *Dead-End*, p. 349.
7. *Walker v. First Presbyterian Church*, 22 Fair Empl. Prac. 762 (Cal. Super. 1980).
8. *Gay Rights Coalition v. Georgetown University*, 536 A2d 1 (D.C. App. 1987).
9. *Employment Div., Dep't of Human Resources v. Smith*, 110 S. Ct. 1595, 1990).
10. George F. Will, "College, Religion and Gays: How 'Rights' Threaten Freedom," in the *Los Angeles Times*.

Chapter 13—Dismantling the Nuclear Family
1. Beverly Beyette, "Describing a 'Family' by Function, Not Form," in the *Los Angeles Times*, Dec. 3, 1989.
2. Ibid.
3. Judy Anderson, "What is 'Family'?" in *The Vancouver Sun*, Dec. 1, 1992, Editorial, p. A13.
4. "World of Gay Couples," in *Parade Magazine*, Feb. 5, 1984, p. 8.
5. Ibid.
6. Elaine Herscher, "Domestic Partners Celebrate," in the *San Francisco Chronicle*, Feb. 14, 1992, Final Ed., p. A25.
7. Mark Poggioli, "Letters to the Editor," in the *San Francisco Chronicle*, Dec. 17, 1990, Editorial, p. A16.
8. George F. Will, "Reading and writing and nonoxynol-9," syndicated by Washington Post Writers Group.
9. Michael Willhoite, *Daddy's Roommate* (Boston: Alyson Publications, 1991).
10. Ibid.
11. Ibid.
12. Ibid.
13. "Ruling on Lesbian 'Spouse' Applauded," in the *Los Angeles Times*, Oct. 8, 1991.
14. *Education Week*, May 18, 1988.
15. "Gay Rights at Work," in the *California Lawyer*, Sep. 1984, p. 49.
16. Ibid.
17. Ibid.
18. Ibid.
19. *San Francisco Chronicle*, Aug. 7, 1992, Final Ed., News, p. A21.
20. "Fostering Prejudice," transcript from Heart of the Matter, program transmitted 14th February 1993, BBC, London.
21. Richard John Neuhaus, *The Naked Public Square*, 2nd ed. (Grand Rapids: Eerdmans Publishing Company, 1984), p. 96.
22. Usdansky, "Gay couples," p. 8A.
23. Neuhaus, *Square*, p. 97.
24. Ibid.

Chapter 14—The Myths About Heterosexual AIDS
1. "Women Living With AIDS," *Oprah*, transcript of Feb. 18, 1987, p. 2, as quoted in Michael Fumento, *The Myth of Heterosexual AIDS*, p. 3.

2. Jenny Rees, "Cut AIDS research urges economist," in *The Daily Telegraph*, June 14, 1991.
3. *The Jerusalem Post*, Aug. 31, 1989, Features.
4. Mona Charen, "The Curious Ways of AIDS Activists," in *Newsday*, Jan. 22, 1992, Wednesday, City Ed., Viewpoints, p. 76.
5. Merle A. Sande, M.D. and Paul A. Volberding, M.D., *The Medical Management of AIDS* (Philadelphia: W. B. Saunders Company, 1988), p. 20.
6. "Study of Brothel Prostitutes Finds Little Venereal Disease," in the *Los Angeles Times*, Aug. 26, 1991, Part A, p. 3; "Legalized Prostitution," in *The Economist*, Sep. 7, 1991, American Survey, p. 28.
7. Denise Grady et al, "Just How *Does* AIDS Spread?" in *Time*, Mar. 21, 1988, p. 61.
8. Sande and Volberding, ibid.
9. Green, *Dead-End*, p. 99.
10. John Seale, M.D., MRCP, "The Aids Epidemic and its Control," in the *British Medico-Chirurgical Journal*, Vol. 102 (iii), Aug. 1987, p. 66.
11. "Why the Course of AIDS is Defying Africa's Precedent", in the *New York Times*, Feb. 21, 1988, Late City Final Ed., Sec. 4, p. 6.
12. Neville Hodgkinson, "Epidemic of Aids in Africa 'a tragic myth,'" in *The Sunday Times* (London), Mar. 21, 1993, News 2 .
13. Ibid.
14. Ibid.
15. Joan Shenton, "AIDS and Africa," in *Dispatches*, Channel 4 (London) programme aired Mar. 24, 1993.
16. Ibid.
17. Ibid.
18. Ibid.
19. Ibid.
20. Ibid.
21. Ibid.
22. Hodgkinson, "Epidemic."
23. Ibid.
24. John Seale, M.D., in *The Daily Telegraph*, Nov. 1986.
25. Hodgkinson, "Epidemic."
26. Shenton, "AIDS and Africa."
27. Rhonda M. Robinson, "AIDS: The Mismanagement of a Tragedy," paper presented in Law and Morality seminar, Pepperdine University, Fall 1990.
28. Michael Fumento, *The Myth of Heterosexual Aids* (New York: Basic Books, Inc., 1990).
29. Deirdre Fernand and Jasper Gerard, "Don't Believe the Hype," in the *Sunday Times* (London), Mar. 1, 1992, Features; *Sunday Telegraph* (London), Mar. 11, 1990, p. 21.
30. Patricia Cohen, "The Myth of Heterosexual AIDS" (book review in the *Washington Monthly*, Nov. 1989).
31. Auberon Waugh, "The dollar dimension," in *The Daily Telegraph*, Feb. 17, 1993, p. 21.
32. Hodgkinson, "Epidemic."
33. Shenton, "AIDS and Africa."
34. Ibid.
35. Charen, "Curious Ways."
36. Ibid.
37. Ibid.
38. Michael Fumento, "What You Can Do to Avoid AIDS," in the *Washington Monthly*, Dec. 1992, Vol. 24, No. 12, p. 46.
39. Rees, "Cut AIDS."
40. Cohen, "Myth."
41. James Kilpatrick, "Encouraging safe sodomy," in Universal Press Syndicate, Nov. 14, 1987.
42. Fumento, "Avoid."

Chapter 15—Manifesto for Sexual Sanity
1. Adam Nagourney, *The New Republic*, Jan. 4, 1993, Vol. 208, No. 1-2, p. 16.
2. 1 Samuel 8:4-22.
3. Statement on Ballot Measure 9, by Most Reverend William J. Levada, Archbishop of Portland, President of Oregon Catholic Conference; and Most Reverend Thomas J. Connolly, Bishop of Baker, Vice-President of Oregon Catholic Conference, letter dated Sep. 29, 1992.
4. Philip Ramsdell, Oregon Citizens Alliance, phone interview, Apr. 15, 1993.
5. Matthew 10:16.
6. Matthew 10:15.
7. Ephesians 4:15.
8. Luke 6:27,28.
9. Leslie Kaufman, "Beat the Press," in *The Washington Monthly*, Mar. 1993, p. 35.
10. Ibid.
11. Ibid.
12. Matthew 10:17,18.
13. Matthew 10:22.
14. Matthew 10:28.

Recommended Reading

Joe Dallas. *Desires in Conflict*. Harvest House Publishers, 1991.

Guide to understanding the root causes of homosexual orientation and how one's behavior patterns can be changed.

Stephen Green. *The Sexual Dead-End*. Broadview Books, 1992.

The definitive work on the gay-rights movement in Britain. Available from: Broadview Books, P.O. Box 782, London SW16 2YT, England.

Roger J. Magnuson. *Are Gay Rights Right?* Multnomah Press, 1988.

Overview of the gay-rights movement with emphasis on the impact of homosexuals on health care, law, and education.